Thought is
Your Enemy

Thought is Your Enemy

(Conversations with U.G. Krishnamurti)

Foreword by
MAHESH BHATT

Editors
ANTONY PAUL FRANK NORONHA
J.S.R.L. NARAYANA MOORTY
SUNITA PANT BANSAL

Smriti Books
New Delhi (INDIA)

*My teaching, if that is the word you want to use,
has no copyright. You are free to reproduce,
distribute, interpret, misinterpret, distort, garble,
do what you like, even claim authorship,
without my consent or the permission of anybody.*

U.G.

ISBN: 81-87967-11-0

First Edition: *2002*

© Design and Presentation: Smriti Books
Cover Design: Rathin Sengupta
Pictures: Courtesy Julie Thayer

Publishers
SMRITI BOOKS
124, Siddhartha Enclave,
New Delhi-110 014 (INDIA)
Email: sunitapb@hotmail.com
Website: www.spbenterprises.com

Distributors
NEW AGE BOOKS
A-44 Naraina Phase I
New Delhi-110 028 (INDIA)
Email: nab@vsnl.in
Website: www.newagebooksindia.com

Printed in India
by Jainendra Prakash Jain at Shri Jainendra Press
A-45 Naraina Phase-I New Delhi-110 028 (INDIA)

Publisher's Note

When I gave the printer's dummy of U.G.'s first book, *The Courage to Stand Alone*, to Mahesh Bhatt, he remarked: "Devastating, isn't he?" I mumbled, "No, I think the book is very good. What he is saying is correct." It was our first meeting, Mahesh was in the middle of a shoot and I did not want to disturb him any further, but, what I actually wanted to say was, U.G.'s statements are devastating only for those who shun the truth. In Hindi, we do have a saying that the truth is always bitter. The trouble is that most of us do not like bitter things.

Thought is Your Enemy is another such truth. Superficially speaking, have you ever wondered why the animals seem to be happier and healthier? They do not think like us. We are also aware of the rising incidence of stress related disorders, all stemming from our thoughts. This is just the tip of the iceberg.

This book explores a very wide spectrum of issues related to thought. Try reaching the depths of these conversations and you shall certainly find some pearls of wisdom.

Contents

Foreword

"Are you watching it on television?" asked a friend who works for the Associated Press. "What?" I asked, least expecting what he was about to say. "The World Trade Center in New York City has been blown up." Seconds later as I watched the symbol of United State's prosperity and supremacy crumble to the ground, into a smouldering heap of dust. I was reminded of U.G. and the conversation I had with him in the summer of 1995, in Gstaad, Switzerland. "Your mind poses as much a threat to the future of mankind as the nuclear weapon. The hydrogen bomb was born the day the cave man used the jawbone of an ass to kill his neighbour. Today when the twentieth century is about to end, your so-called civilized man is still doing what the caveman did but he says he is doing it for the 'good of mankind.' All those who claim that that they are on the side of Right and Justice and will burn away the evil of others are the real enemies of mankind. How does it matter, Mahesh how the world chooses to blow itself up. What difference does it make whether the bomb has the markings of the stars and stripes or a hammer and sickle or a crescent or a Jewish star or the Ashok Chakra?

The U.S.A. should thank Hitler for what it is today. The Second World War gave a major boost to its war industry. But enough is enough! The United States and the industrial nations have ganged up and bullied the rest of the world for too long. They have to be stopped in their tracks and this, I'm afraid, will be done only by the Islamic fundamentalists!"

So, on the night of 11th September, 2001 as I sat glued to my television, switching from CNN to BBC and then to our own ZEE News and Doordarshan, I could clearly see that U.G.'s prophecy had come true. In the vigorous dawn of the 21st century the world was heading towards complete and total annihilation. That too under the name of 'God.' I wondered why men who 'love' their God excessively force others to love that God too? And if they refuse, why do they too eagerly exterminate them?

"Do you believe in God?" I had once asked U.G. "That messy thing called the mind has created many destructive things," he said, "and by far the most destructive of them all is God. To me the question of God is irrelevant and immaterial." He raged, "We have no use for God. More people have been killed in the name of God than in the two world wars put together. In Japan, millions of people died in the name of the sacred Buddha. Even in India, five thousand Jains were massacred in a single day. Yours is not a peaceful nation! Read your own history—it's full of violence from the beginning to the end. Man is merely a biological being. There is no spiritual side to his nature. All the virtues, principles, beliefs, ideas and spiritual values are mere affectations. They haven't succeeded in changing anything in you. You're still the brute that you have always been. When will you begin to see the truth that the philosophy of 'Love thy neighbour as thyself' is not what stops you from killing indiscriminately but it's the terror of the fact that if you kill your neighbour you too will also be destroyed along with him that stops you from killing."

On the 7th of October, 2001, the swashbuckling United States of America in order to recover its tattered national honour bombed Afghanistan. What was distressing was that the bloodletting was sanctioned and legislated for by the highest civil authorities of the world community and it had the consent of the vast majority of the world population. Throughout history ordinary men and women have rejoiced as they watched man batter man and cheered at those grotesque acts of cruelty. This association of pleasure with cruelty and killing is shocking but familiar and the world was getting ready to have a belly full of entertainment. Like the 100-day battle of the U.S.A. against Iraq in 1991, this war too was going to be video-game war, a televised display of high-tech weaponry that would bring dramatic images of remote combat into the living rooms of television audiences world-over in record setting numbers. The tragedy of a war-weary Afghanistan was being turned into global entertainment.

"This war will go on forever..." said U.G. when I called him in Switzerland on the night of 11th September. "Don't expect this to stop after a few months or a few years like the wars of the last century. This is a new kind of war. Mankind will never win the war against drugs and terrorism. This is the age in which you can cause maximum damage through minimum means. Beware, the day is not very far when these people whom you call 'terrorists' will get hold of your nuclear arsenal. The western nations will sing a different song the day that happens."

On the 15th of October 2001, the threat of Bio-terrorism, something that had till now felt like a nightmare that would never visit America, entered its shores. News of a possible Anthrax attack, by means of the U.S. mail in several places including the office of a Senator sent shudders of anxiety and anger across the country. As I watched a 'moon-suited' worker swabbing for

samples of the killer germ on CNN, I called U.G. who was at that
time in Palm Springs, California to get a first-hand account of how
serious the situation was in the U. S.

" The Anthrax attacks are spreading all over the United States.
The authorities are trying to suppress this fact and doing all they
can to play it down. Calling the Americans 'paranoid' would be
describing them in very mild terms. They are probably taping our
phone conversation at this very moment! So don't say anything
subversive. You will get into trouble. The "Enduring Freedom"
this country claims to be fighting for, does not operate here. This
is not the land of the brave and the home of the free! The United
States of America has become a Police State! I will probably get
out of here in a week's time. I don't know where I will go next.
But one thing is certain I don't want to set my foot in India. You
know why? Because you have opened the doors to the
Americans! They have started a civil war in Pakistan and soon
they will turn Kashmir into another Middle East. That great heritage
you all are very proud of has produced spineless people like your
leaders who do not have the guts to ask the western nations to get
out!"

It is impossible for me to communicate the authority with which
he said what he said. His tone had a sense of finality that made me
shiver. I know that his intention was not to evoke some kind of
paranoia within me. It was to awaken me fiercely. And before he
hung up, he said something that will stay with me till my dying day.
He said, "Mahesh individually you cannot do anything to change
the course of events that are taking place in Afghanistan today.
And collective action means war. If you stand up to oppose the
Powers-that-Be then you will become their enemy and they will
finish you. Man can't do anything but destroy himself and everything
that nature has built around him . Man is the worst species existing

on this planet. And all he is destined to do is push mankind in the direction of total destruction."

Mahesh Bhatt
Mumbai, India
2001

From U.G.

There is no teaching of mine, and never shall be one. 'Teaching' is not the word for it. 'Teaching' implies a method or a system, a technique or a new way of thinking to be applied in order to bring about a transformation in your way of life. What I am saying is outside the field of teachability; it is simply a description of the way I am functioning. It is just a description of the natural state of man – that is the way you, stripped of the machinations of thought, are also functioning.

The natural state is not the state of a self-realized or God-realized man, it is not a thing to be achieved or attained, it is not a thing to be willed into existence; it is there – it is the living state. This state is just the functional activity of life. By "life" I do not mean something abstract; it is the life of the senses, functioning naturally without the interference of thought. Thought is an interloper, which thrusts itself into the affairs of the senses. It has a profit motive: thought directs the activity of the senses to get something out of them and uses them to give itself continuity.

Your natural state has no relationship whatsoever with the religious states of bliss, beatitude; and ecstasy; they lie within the field of experience. Those who have led man on his search for religiousness throughout the centuries have perhaps experienced those religious states. So can you. They are thought-induced states of being, and as they come, so do they go. They can never be grasped, contained, much less given expressions to, by any man. That beaten track will lead you nowhere. There is no oasis situated yonder; you are stuck with the mirage.

U.G.

Preface

If you think that you can read and understand this book, you may be quite off the mark. "Anybody who comes and listens to me and tries to understand what I am trying to put across is wasting his time, because there is no way you can listen to anything without interpretation," says U.G. Krishnamurti.

According to him, when we leave the sense of hearing alone, all that is there is the vibration of sounds. These vibrations are picked up by the eardrum, transferred to the nerves that run to the brain, and are interpreted according to what he calls 'our reference point'. Thus we hear our own translations of the vibrations, says U.G., "That is all right for a relationship with someone on the level of 'Here is some money; give me half a kilo of carrots'; but that is the limit of your relationship, of your communication with anybody".

Whether you agree or not with all that he says, it is really worth a try to listen to him. The words that come out of him are like grenades lobbed into our 'reference point', threatening to uproot everything we believed in. His statements are devastating, more so to people who are nurtured in a religious atmosphere.

U.G. can also discuss quantum physics and black holes, and eros and thanatos. U.G. says, "I do not claim to have a special insight into the nature of things or that I understand the workings of nature more than anybody else. But this is what I discovered for myself. I do not care whether you accept what I am saying or not. It stands or falls by itself". His statements have a solid ring of authenticity and seem to spring from a source other than thinking. What he says shakes the very foundation of human thought.

The story of U.G. Krishnamurti has all the ingredients of a thriller. One episode in his life leads to another without any systematic sequence. When he reached the age of forty-nine, there was sudden turn of events. Something happened to him which he called a "calamity" (to help our understanding), when he stumbled upon a "natural state", wherein, in his words, "everything that man had said, felt, or seen, in fact, the whole heritage of mankind was thrown out of my system".

But, according to U.G., this was not what he desired. He was looking for a spiritual dreamland waxed eloquent by the holy men – frauds as well as genuine. The religious atmosphere was part of his background. U.G. was born in 1918 into a middle class Brahmin family in Andhra Pradesh. His mother died soon after giving birth to him. On her deathbed she said her child was cut out for something "immeasurably high". U.G.'s grandfather took her words seriously and groomed him in an ascetic atmosphere.

A small episode, however, was a turning point in U.G.'s life. His grandfather was once meditating early in the morning when he was disturbed by the cries of a child. The old man was so angry that he beat the child black and blue. The incongruity and brutality of the scene had a traumatic impact on the tender sensibilities of U.G. He said to himself, "If this is what meditation is about, it is worthless" and threw away his sacred thread.

U.G.'s life thereafter was an experiment with truth. An insatiable hunger overtook him to find out whether there was anything behind the abstract pronouncements of the so-called spiritual men. He met various masters including J. Krishnamurti and Ramana Maharshi and practiced traditional meditations. He exhausted every means possible to reach the "promised land" and at the end was bereft of hope and thrown into utter despair.

On his forty-ninth birthday he was sitting on a bench overlooking the green valley and rugged peaks of Oberland in Switzerland. It suddenly occurred to him, "I have searched everywhere to find an answer to my question, 'Is there enlightenment?' but I have never questioned the search itself, because I have assumed that enlightenment exists and that I have to reach for it. However, it is the search itself which has been choking me and keeping me out of my natural state".

He said to himself, "There is no such thing as spiritual or psychological enlightenment, because there is no such thing as spirit or psyche at all. I have been a fool all my life, searching for something that does not exist. My search is at an end". His voracious hunger to find the fairyland promised by the prophets and spiritual masters had burnt itself out. The occurrence had telling effects on his body. Many physical changes took place within him, which bewildered the medical men and friends around him. His life thereafter became one in which there was "no thought for the morrow nor grief over the past".

According to U.G., grief and joy exist only in the realm of the mind. The body is interested in neither. Its only interest is in surviving the day-to-day challenges it encounters from moment to moment.

U.G.'s statements are enigmatic; his words defy the logical framework, which we are accustomed to. U.G. dismisses the possibility of any experience except through knowledge. According to him, it is knowledge that creates experience, and it is the experience, which in turn strengthens the knowledge. 'Knowledge' does not have any metaphysical or epistemological overtones. It is simply that something is a chair or a table, or that some sensation is pleasurable or painful. In fact, even the process of recognition and naming of something is part of knowledge. The total operation is designated 'thinking'.

What distinguishes us from U.G. is that this knowledge which is operating through the process of thinking is in a declutched state in U.G., while there is a constant undercurrent of thinking activity within us, whether we like it or not. Our mind is constantly churning out thought after thought in various shapes, colours, and size. U.G. says that it is through this constant thinking that we are maintaining the continuity of what we call the 'I' or 'self'.

In U.G. continuity of thought has been snapped. Thoughts come to him in a disjointed manner without any link-up. He thinks only when there is a demand for experience. Otherwise, what there is is only the simple activity of the senses – the stimulus-and-response continuum. Since it is the continuous thinking activity that gives the illusion of the 'self' or 'I', there is no feeling of 'self' or 'I' within him.

U.G. says the stranglehold on the physical organism of what is called knowledge has the potency of millions of years. The knowledge, which operates in the form of thought, has set up a parallel empire of its own, in contradistinction to the ways of nature. But thought subtly "knows" its ephemeral nature, and the fear of its fleeting existence propels it to erect a marvellous structure of culture, civilization, religion, politics, the various institutions and values that govern our lives, and, in fact, everything that we can conceive of.

All these facets of human life are nothing but props through which thought tries to enthrone itself in permanence. In other words, what we call 'I' or 'you' is thought seeking permanence in innumerable activities. U.G. says that only when, by some miracle or strange chance, the living organism is freed from the stranglehold of the empire created by thought, can the body, with its extraordinary intelligence, free the human being so that he can "fall" into his "natural state". According to U.G., one cannot use one's volition or go through any rigorous discipline to come into the natural state. Such a state is beyond the field of experience. U.G. often describes his situation thus: "How did it all happen? I don't know. What is it that has happened? I don't know. Has anything happened at all?" He says that what has happened to him is such that it cannot be shared with anybody, and that the natural state cannot be expressed or contained in thought.

What is the so – called "natural state" to people who are not functioning in it? Mortals who are looking for a panacea to all their problems ask the question from a non-natural-state perspective. Peace and happiness are what we are all after, and U.G.'s "natural state" offers us no experience of anything like it. So what we are left with are our points of view about the person, depending on our prejudices and conditioning. Call him a fraud or a freak of nature, but once you are anywhere near the vortex of U.G.'s presence you are left dumbfounded. Your expectations and opinions are shattered. You are left to wonder as to what is the source from which his statements spring. Beneath his apparent human form there lies something which defies description.

Antony Paul Frank Noronha
New Delhi

No Mind, No Soul, Only the Body

*All insights, however extraordinary they may be,
are worthless, because it is thought that has created what we call insight, and through that, it is
maintaining its continuity and status quo.*

**Q : U.G. I would like to probe into the very essence of
your revolutionary and uncompromising statement, "There
is no soul".**

U.G.: There is no self, there is no I, there is no spirit, there is
no soul, and there is no mind. That knocks off the whole list, and
you have no way of finding out what you are left with. You may
very well ask me the question, "Why do you go on telling people
about the way you are functioning"? It is only to emphasize that
we have been for centuries using some instrument, that is, thinking
or mind, or whatever you want to call it, to free ourselves from
the whole of what you call the 'I', or the 'self', and all kinds of
things. That is what the whole quest of spirit is all about. But when
once it dawns on you that there is nothing to be free from, then

these questions don't arise at all. How that dawned on me, I have no way of finding out for myself.

Q : Ordinary human beings like me would like to know if you could find answers for us.

U.G.: The answers I give are only to emphasize that what we are left with is the functioning of the living organism. How it is functioning is all that I am trying to put across, emphasize, and overemphasize all the time. My interest is to somehow make you see that the whole attempt on your part to understand what you are left with is a lost battle.

Q : But I want to probe around this...

U.G.: The more the questions you throw at me the more there is a need to emphasize the physical aspect of your existence, namely, that there is nothing to what we have been made to believe. All our problems have arisen because of our acceptance that it is possible for us to understand the reality of the world, or the reality of our existence. What I am saying is that you have no way of experiencing anything that you do not know. So anything that you have experienced through the help of your knowledge is fruitless. It is a lost battle.

Q : When you are saying that there is no non-physical element in human nature...

U.G.: I am not with you. What exactly do you mean when you say, "No non-physical element in human nature"?

Q : I mean that there is only the actual physical body and the world as it is.

U.G.: That is the reason why I say that the instrument which we are using to understand the reality of our existence and the reality of the world around us is not part of this [body] mechanism that is there. That is the reason why I say thoughts are not self-generated and are not spontaneous. There are no thoughts there even now. If you want to find out whether there is any such thing as thought, the very question that we are posing to ourselves, namely, "Is there a thought?" is born out of the assumption that there is a thought there. But what you will find there is all *about* thought and *not* thought. All *about* thought is what is put in there by the culture. It is put in by the people who are telling us that it is very essential for you to free yourself from whatever you are trying to free yourself from through the instrument. My interest is to emphasize that, that is not the instrument, and there is no other instrument. And when once this hits you, dawns upon you that thought is not the instrument, and that there is no other instrument, then there is no need for you to find out if any other instrument is necessary. No need for any other instrument. This very same structure that we are using, the instrument which we are using, has in a very ingenious way invented all kinds of things like intuition, right insight, right this, that, and the other. And to say that through this very insight we have come to understand something is the stumbling block. All insights, however extraordinary they may be, are worthless, because it is thought that has created what we call insight, and through that it is maintaining its continuity and status quo.

Q : I think I understand that, but what I want to pursue is that there is the physical side of this, and if I could observe clearly the human organism there and its interrelated functions...

U.G.: As a matter of fact even that is not possible to experience and understand except through the knowledge that is given to us by the physiologists.

Q : You mean our own observation...?

U.G.: There is no such thing as your own observation. Your own observation is born out of the knowledge that you have. This knowledge comes from the physiologists. This knowledge comes from those who have been involved in medical technology. They are trying to find out how this body is functioning, how the heart is functioning, and a whole lot of things that we have become familiar with, though what they have discovered is something which cannot be experienced by us.

Q : What you are saying then is that there is really no such thing as direct or immediate experience...

U.G.: There is no experience at all without the help of knowledge. That is all that I am saying. There is no way you can experience the reality of anything except through the help of this knowledge. So what I am saying is that you cannot experience what you do not know. Therefore, you project that there is something beyond the mechanism of the experiencing structure. There is no 'beyond'. But that 'beyond' is again affirmed or rejected by this experiencing structure to maintain its continuity. It is a game.

Q : Back to that. I asked you this before. Isn't there an experience of touch?

U.G.: No. The only way you can even experience the sense of touch is through this contact; that is what you call the sense of touch. So you are bringing your fingers here and touching it here. [*He touches the arm of the chair.*] The eye is looking at it. But it does not translate the movement of that as somebody putting his finger here to know what exactly happens when you touch this. The eye cannot say that, and the sense of touch does not translate that for any reason. Unless you ask the question...

Q : I am suggesting that...

U.G.: The eye is looking at it.

Q : No, I am not looking at it.

U.G.: You are not.

Q : I can feel, I can feel without...

U.G.: It is born out of your imagination and translation of this particular tactile sensing within the framework of your past experience. At this moment if that is not translated as a soft touch, or a hard touch, or even as a touch of your hand, you have no way of separating the two and experiencing that.

Q : No more separating the two...

U.G.: Supposing you ask me a question for whatever reason that you want to know, the sole knowledge you have is here in the computer [*pointing to his head*], and it comes out and tells me and tells you that you are touching this, and that the sense of touch is translating that as the soft touch of the friend who is sitting next to me.

Q : I might be walking alone, and I feel a breeze coming. I am not doing anything, but it is blowing in my way.

U.G.: If you do not translate the breeze touching your body...

Q : I am feeling the breeze.

U.G.: The feeling is also a thought. The moment you separate yourself from the breeze, that sensory activity is translated within the framework of the knowledge you already have. I am not for a moment saying that you *are* the breeze. What I am saying is that all you are saying is part of the knowledge you have. Otherwise there is no way you can separate the breeze and the body.

Q : So you are saying that there is no such thing as a new experience.

U.G.: There is no new experience at all. But the demand to experience the same thing over and over again is the one that is wearing off the whole mechanism of memory for purposes for which it is not intended.

Q : Is it possible for us to see that memory should not be the operative factor in consciousness?

U.G.: I question consciousness because what we call consciousness is memory. You become conscious of something through the help of the knowledge you have, and that knowledge is locked up in the memory. So the whole talk of the subconscious, unconscious, levels of consciousness, and all that, is the ingenious invention of the thinking mechanism. Through this cleverness, inventiveness, it maintains its continuity.

Q : Do you make any distinction between awareness and consciousness?

U.G.: Awareness has no meaning to me because awareness is not an instrument to be used to understand anything, much less to bring about a change there. First of all, there is nothing there to be changed. Since there is nothing there to be changed, whether you use awareness or any other instrument to bring about a change is irrelevant. Awareness can never be separated from the activity of the brain. That is the reason why I always describe what is happing here [*pointing to himself*] in physical terms. "The reflection of that, [*pointing to a cushion*] whatever it is, on the retina, and to experience that without naming it", is only a clever game we are playing with ourselves. You think that recognition is separate from naming. This is not true. Recognition and naming are one and the same. Whether I name it or not, the very recognition of you as a man or that as a pillow itself means that the naming is already there. That is the reason why I point out to the people who say that the word is *not* the thing, the word *is* the thing. If the word is not the thing, what the hell is it? It is all right for the philosophers to sit and discuss everlastingly that the word is not the thing. That implies that there is something there other than the word. So you cannot accept the fact that the word *is* the object. That is, even if you say that there is an object without using the word, it means that there is a separation there. What I am trying to tell you is how this division, separation is occurring.

Q : Separation is really the beginning of duality.

U.G.: I never tell myself and tell you that I am the table. That is too absurd. So what I am saying is that there is no way you can separate yourself on your own free will and volition except when there is demand from outside. You ask the question, "What is that"? You and I have the same information in our memories. Whether you use the French word, an English word, a German word, or a Latin word, it doesn't matter. The reference point is the table you are asking me about. So, I say it is a table, and that it is a white table. You and I have the same information. When that question is not there, I would at no time look at it and tell myself that it is a table. It does not mean that I am 'choicelessly aware' of that. What is there is only the reflection of this object on the retina. I cannot experience even this statement, because the stimulus and response are one unitary movement. The moment you say there is awareness, there is already a division.

Q : Why do we maintain this position, this duality and this separation…?

U.G.: That is the only way you can continue. Otherwise you are coming to an end. The *you* as you know yourself, the *you* as you experience yourself, that *you* is the identity there. Through the constant demand for using memory it maintains its continuity. If that 'you' is not there, you don't know what will happen. That is why the phrase, "freedom from the known" is very attractive up to a point. Once you are free from the known, there is no way you can say anything about it. So, if I am listening to somebody like you who is talking about the need to have the freedom from the known, your emphasis that there is a need to free yourself from the known has already become part of the known. Thought has survived for millions and millions of years, and it knows every trick in the world. It will do anything to maintain its continuity.

Q : So thinking has really no place in understanding …

U.G.: There is no thinking at all. If there is no thinker, there are no thoughts at all. You cannot say there is only thought and there is no thinker. The thoughts do not come from here [*pointing to his head*], they are coming from outside. The translation of a sensory perception within the framework of your experiencing structure is thought. And you are using those thoughts to achieve a goal.

Q : I have got to know about this thinking. This is sequential …

U.G.: No, you can try that. I am not your teacher. What is happening here is a mechanical thing like in a computer. It is mechanically operating, trying to find out if there is any information stored in the computer [*pointing to his head*] related to what we are talking about. "Let me see", "Let me think"; these are statements you are just making, but there is no further activity and no thinking taking place there. You have an illusion that there is somebody who is thinking and bringing out the information. Look, this is no different from the extraordinary instrument we have, the word-finder. You press a button and "Ready", it says. Then you ask for a word; "Searching", it says. That searching is thinking. But it is a mechanical process. In the word-finder or computer there is no thinker. There is no thinker thinking at all. If there is any information or anything that is referred to, the computer puts it together and throws it out. That is all that is happening. It is a very mechanical thing that is happening. We are not ready to accept that thought is mechanical because that knocks off the whole image that we are not just machines. It is an extraordinary machine. It is not different from the computers that we use. But this [*pointing to his body*] is something living; it has got a living quality to it. It has vitality. It is not just mechanically repeating; it carries with it the life energy like that current energy.

Q : One of the things that human beings use most often is imagination ...

U.G.: The idea that you experience the totality of your body is born out of your imagination. Actually, there is no way you can experience the totality of it. Your experience of the heaviness of your body is due to the gravitational force. Sometimes you experience the heaviness of your body when thoughts are not in operation. Sometimes thoughts slow down in everybody. That is the time when you feel heavier than the heaviest object. You feel as if you weigh 640 kilos, or suddenly feel as if you are walking on air. These are the actual functioning of the body, which they have described in some spiritual terms and given so much importance to.

Q : So, people in this area of imagination think that unfettered thinking can sometimes come with new possibilities, of ways in which you can live more fruitfully, more easily or more pleasurably...

U.G.: That is something that is not valid and true.

Q : This is what people assume. If one has an opportunity to do that, one can do so. What is wrong with that?

U.G.: See, it works in certain areas. You know, we have a mathematical problem, we are thinking about it. You come out with an answer and say that this is the product of your thinking. But sometimes you exhaust all the possibilities, the variations and combinations of finding out the solution of a particular mathematical problem or a scientific problem. You are so tired that you go to sleep. But when you wake up the answer is there. This is possible in the area of mathematical problems. Thinking cannot help us solve living problems. There is no way we can use that to solve human problems. That is why it has failed to solve our problems. It has not touched anything here [*pointing to his body*]. All our beliefs have not touched anything here. We don't know what we would do in a given situation. You can say that you are going to be a non-violent man. But what you would do in a given situation you would never know. The demand to be prepared for all future actions and situations is the cause of our problems. Every situation is so different, that our preparedness to meet the situation with the knowledge we have of answering and dealing with situations cannot help us.

Q : Then what does the phrase "living challenge" mean?

U.G.: I don't know, the way you are putting questions...

Q : You meet a new situation...

U.G.: It is not a challenge. The inadequacy of using what you have, preparing yourself, and the question of how to deal with the situation is absent here. It ceases to be a challenge then. That is why I say there are no problems there. We create the problems. If the solutions we are offered by the people are really not the solutions, you really don't have the problem. But the fact of the matter is, if you do not have a problem, you create a problem. You cannot live without problems.

Q : That is right. What you are saying in one sense is that the human being is not really different from animals.

U.G.: I must admit that we are probably far more evolved than the other animals. That is an advantage to us in functioning in a much better way. I don't like to use the word "better", but rather, "in a more natural way". We are free from some dangers. All these problems can be handled with the highly evolved structure that we have been endowed with. That is why what we call psychic powers – clairvoyance, clairaudience, etc. – are already there in the animals. We also have them in us. In the case of some, through techniques of meditation and such gimmicks, thought slows down. Then they experience these so-called powers temporarily, and they think that they are all spiritual experiences. Probably in our case the mechanism is more sensitive than in the case of animals. I don't know; I cannot make any definitive statement. There is no way you can really understand how animals are functioning. All these gimmicks, all these ideas of experiencing your birth again, rebirthing, this, that, and other things – they are absolute rubbish, because you are trying to go back to the time of your birth and experience your own birth from this point. What you are experiencing is not the experience of your birth, but something from where you are. You use all these experiences, colour them, and imagine that you are experiencing your own birth. This is good for marketing their "rebirth", but there is nothing to it.

Q : Why is it that human beings have developed some traits which have made them masterful destroyers of the earth, the air, the water, and everything around them?

U.G.: As I said the last time, this separateness from the totality of things around us, and the idea that the whole thing is created for our benefit and that we are created for a grander and nobler purpose than all the other species on this planet, are the causes of this destruction. This powerful use of thoughts is what is destructive. Thought is a self-protective mechanism. So anything that is born out of thought is destructive – whether it is religious thought or scientific thought or political thought – all of them are destructive. But we are not ready to accept that it is thought that is our enemy. We don't know how to function in this world without the use of thought. You can invent all kinds of things and try to free yourself from this stranglehold of thought, but there is no way we can accept the fact that that is not the instrument to help us to function sanely and intelligently in this world. Thought is a self-perpetuating mechanism. It controls, moulds, and shapes our ideas and actions. Idea and action – they are one and the same. All our actions are born out of ideas. Our ideas are thoughts passed on to us from generation to generation. Thought is not the instrument to help us to live in harmony with the life around us. That is why you create all these ecological problems, problems of pollution, and the problem of possibly destroying ourselves with the most destructive weapons that we have invented. So, there is no way out. You may say that I am a pessimist, that I am a cynic, or that I am this, that, and the other. But I hope one day we will realize that the mistakes we have made will destroy everything. The planet is not in danger. We are in danger.

Q : If we are, then we can go to another planet. The desire to survive – whence comes this desire to survive beyond the death of the body and its inevitable demise?

U.G.: Because you know in a way that what you know of yourself is coming to an end there. You have lived sixty, seventy, or a hundred years of your life; you have been through so many experiences; you have achieved so many things; you have attained and accomplished so many things. "Is all that coming to an end – leaving behind nothing"? So, naturally we create something 'beyond'.

Q : Why do you think that what we have allowed an illusion and unreality to persist in consciousness or human thought...?

U.G.: You are not separate from that illusion. You *are* the illusion. If one illusion goes, it is always replaced with another illusion. Why? Because, the ending of the illusion is the ending of *you*. That is the death. The ending of belief is the ending of the 'you' that is there. So, that is not the poetic, romantic death of "dying to your yesterdays". Physical death is the only way through which you flush out what your whole culture has put in there.

Q : In a smaller and minor way, I can *see* through an illusion...

U.G.: That is another illusion. The illusion is that "the seeing is the ending". There is no way you can separate yourself and the seeing. Seeing is the illusion; the seer is the illusion. The seer tells himself that "seeing is ending", but it does not end. So the seer does not want to come to an end. The seer is the illusion. I don't know; it is better not to discuss these things. Through the invention of what is called "the seeing of the illusion is the ending", the seer is gathering momentum and continuing. The moment you want to 'see' something you have separated yourself from that and the seer has come into being, and through that seeing he is maintaining his continuity. That is why seeing has not helped us; it has ended nothing there.

Q : This dialogue, our talking together now – what would you like to call it? Is it just a physical exchange... this interplay that is going on now?

U.G.: *Laughs.* I don't really want to repeat again and again. This is just a puppet sitting here. And, two puppets, two computers, two tape recorders playing; that is all.

Q : Whatever you are saying – listening to you, will it not bring about a change in us?

U.G.: Not at all. You are not even listening. There is no such thing as the art of listening. You are not listening at all. Listening is not in your interest. You are interpreting.

Q : I am aware of that. Surely there is some kind of listening. I am trying to put the key in the door and...

U.G.: We don't have to use all those phrases such as, "I am aware of this, that, and, the other". If you put into practice what they call 'awareness', you will go to the way of Alzheimer's disease, which is hitting everybody. I read it in some magazine that it is hitting everybody. It has hit already the famous musician, what is his name, Frank Sinatra. It is there in one of your papers. He is very young. They mention him as an example of how a person suffering from Alzheimer's disease functions. You have the 'key' there in your hand. But you don't know how to use the key and open the door.

Q : Then really what you are saying is that the body has an enormous intelligence because all its functions go on interplaying beautifully in their own way.

U.G.: Our interest to teach that body something, which it is not interested in, is causing, creating problems for it.

Q : Is there anything else that you would like to say?

U.G.: To say what? I have said a lot now.

Q : You certainly have. Another thing that I wanted to ask you about is physical pain – whether...

U.G.: To leave it alone. If there is pain you take some painkiller. I am saying you should do nothing, and let the body suffer and go through the pain. You are actually adding more to the pain. See, as long as the pain is there, I might as well take a pill and free myself from the pain temporarily, because there is no special charm, spiritual or otherwise, to prove to ourselves and to others we can endure pain. That is not what we are talking about. But what we can do is to leave that pain alone without interfering all the time. We think we know a lot more than this body. We think that we know what is good for the body, and that is why we are creating problems for it. It knows what it wants to know. It doesn't want to learn anything from us. If we understand this simple relationship that thought and the body have, then probably, we will allow the body to function and use thought only for functional purposes. Thought is functional in value, and it cannot help us to achieve any of the goals we have placed before us, or what the culture has placed before us.

Q : Is there no such thing as a physical purpose for pain?

U.G.: It is a healer. Pain is a healing process. But we are paranoid. W are overanxious to see that we don't suffer. I am not saying that you should not get any help that is available to you. There is no point in suffering, like the Christian saints who suffer and don't go to a doctor. That is not what I am saying. In fact, anything we say now is of no use. What we would do in any given situation is anybody's guess.

Let us stop and leave it at that. If you make some sense out of that, than you make it. If you don't, than you simply don't. I wish that nobody remembers anything of what we have discussed so far. If you remember anything, it is lost. Nor am I trying to say that what I say is in a mysterious way affecting the whole of human consciousness.

Q : I do think that pain is really a healer. I am not contradicting what you said, but pain is inborn.

U.G.: It is there. It is trying to heal us because of some disequilibrium. But what I am suggesting is that there is no charm in suffering; some helping hand can be given to make it a little bit bearable. I don't see any point in any kind of suffering. That is all I am saying.

Q : If the pain is in your knee, in your back, or in your head, it is already there...

U.G.: May I say something? Anything that we discuss about pain at this moment has no meaning because we are not having any pain now. If some pain is really there then we wouldn't discuss it; some action would be there.

Q : Yes, that is right.

U.G.: Your value system is the one that is responsible for the human malady, human tragedy, forcing everybody to fit into that model.

Throw Away Your Crutches

A guru is one who tells you to throw away all crutches. He would ask you to walk, and he would say that if you fall, you should rise and walk again.

Q : First of all let us analyze this wonderful notion of happiness in quest of which every human being is on the run. Can you tell us what this happiness is all about?

U.G.: You may not agree with me but when we talk about "the quest for happiness", it is no different from any other sensual activity. As the matter of fact, all experiences, however extraordinary they may be, are in the area of sensuality. That is one major problem that we are facing today. Somewhere along the line, the human species experienced this self-consciousness for the first time. And it separated the human species from the rest of the species on this planet. I don't even know if there is any such thing as evolution, but we are made to believe that there is such a thing. And it was at that time perhaps that thought took its birth. But thought in its birth, in its origin, in its content, in its expression, and in its action is very fascist. When I use the word "fascist" I use it not in the political sense but to mean that thought controls and shapes our thinking and our actions. So it is a very protective mechanism. It has no doubt helped us to be what we are today. It has helped us to create our technology. It has made our life very comfortable. It has also made it possible for us to discover the laws of nature. But thought is a very protective mechanism and is interested in its own survival. At the same time thought is opposed fundamentally to the functioning of this living organism. We are made to believe that there is such a thing as mind. But there is no such thing as your mind or my mind. Society or culture, or whatever you want to call it, has created us solely and wholly for the purpose of maintaining its own continuity and status quo. At the same time, it has also created the idea that there is such a thing as individual. But actually, there is a conflict between the two – the idea of the individual and the impossibility of functioning as an individual separate and distinct from the totality of man's thoughts and experiences.

Q : Who makes us think in a particular way?

U.G.: Here at this point I would like to emphasize that thoughts are not self-generated and spontaneous. I would even go one step further and ask, "Is there any such thing as thought"? The very question arises because we assume that there is such a thing as thought, and that we can separate ourselves from thought and look at it. But when we look at what we call thought, what we see is *about* thought and *not* thought itself. "What is thought"? The question arises only because of the assumption that there is such a thing as thought.

> *We use what we call thought to achieve our spiri-*
> *tual or material goals. We may consider the spiri-*
> *tual goals as "higher". The culture in which we are*
> *functioning places spiritual goals on a higher level*

than the materialistic goals. But the instrument that we are using is matter, which is thought. Thought to me is matter. Therefore, all our spiritual goals are materialistic in their value. And this is the conflict that is going on here. In this process, the totality of man's experiences created what we call a separate identity and a separate mind. But actually if you want to experience anything, be it your own body, or your own experiences, you have no way of experiencing them without the use of knowledge that is passed on to you. In other words, I would say that thought is memory. Everything that is born out of thought is destructive. Anything that we discover, the laws of nature or whatever you call it, is used by us only for destructive purposes. And it is true that we have discovered quite a few of nature's laws, and the theories are constantly changing...

Q : Can we not at least attempt to refine this thought process to make it constructive and positive?

U.G.: Thought is not the instrument for achieving anything other than the goals set before us by our culture or society, or whatever you want to call it. The basic problem we have to face today is this; the cultural input, or what society has placed before us as the goal for all of us to reach and attain, is the enemy of this living organism. Thought can only create problems; it cannot help us to solve any.

Q : Then is it desirable to be thoughtless?

U.G.: What I am talking about is not a thoughtless state. Even the invention of what is called a thoughtless state, placed before us by many spiritual teachers as a goal to be reached, is created by thought so that it can, by pursuing what it calls a thoughtless state, maintain its own continuity. So whatever we experience in this process of achieving the goal of a thoughtless state strengthens and fortifies the very thing that we are trying to be free from.

Q : You see, we have this cause and effect theory that says, "As you sow, so shall you reap". Don't you think that for every action of ours, whether it is thought or any other action, there is a reaction, if not immediately, at least after some time?

U.G.: It is thought that has invented the idea of cause and effect. There may not be any such thing as a cause at all. Every event is an individual and independent event. We link up all these events and try to create a story of our lives. But actually every event is an independent event. If we accept the fact that every event is an independent event in our lives, it creates a tremendous problem of maintaining what we call identity. And identity is the most important factor in our lives. We are able to maintain this identity through the constant use of memory, which is also thought. This constant use of memory or identity, or whatever you call it, is consuming a tremendous amount of energy, and it leaves us with no energy to deal with the problems of our living. Is there is any way that we can free ourselves from the identity? As I said, thought can only create problems; it cannot help us to solve them. Through dialectical thinking about thinking itself we are only sharpening that instrument. All philosophies help us only to sharpen this instrument.

> *Thought is very essential for us to survive in this world. But it cannot help us in achieving the goals that we have placed before ourselves. The goals are unachievable through the help of thought. The quest for happiness, as you mentioned, is impossible because there is no such thing as permanent*

happiness. There are moments of happiness, and there are moments of unhappiness. But the demand to be in a permanent state of happiness is the enemy of this body. This body is interested in maintaining its sensitivity of the sensory perceptions and also the sensitivity of the nervous system. That is very essential for the survival of this body. If we use that instrument of thought for trying to achieve the impossible goal of permanent happiness, the sensitivity of this body is destroyed. Therefore, the body is rejecting all that we are interested in: permanent happiness and permanent pleasure. So, we are not going to succeed in that attempt to be in a permanent state of happiness.

Q : You referred to the intellect and to the sharpening of the intellect...

U.G.: To survive in this world.

Q : Yes. How do we sharpen it? With whose help?

U.G.: Through a repetitive process we are sharpening that instrument. But we are using tremendous amount of energy in this process. If the use of thought is limited to achieve only what we consider to be materialistic values and not our spiritual goals, what is it that is not possible for us in order to function sanely and intelligently. It does not mean that I am teaching a materialistic philosophy or any such thing. Thought is not intended for achieving spiritual goals or even to find out the significance, meaning, or purpose of life, or to be used for the quest for permanence or permanent pleasure.

Q : We have been familiar with the theory of birth and death – karma, action, reaction or something that we bring along with us like a bank balance, add something to it, then spend something, and then carry it forward to the next birth or whatever it is. How far do you subscribe to this theory, or are you opposed to it?

U.G.: I am not opposed to the theory of karma or reincarnation. But I am questioning the very foundation of the belief. There is reincarnation for those who believe in it, and there is no reincarnation for those who do not believe in it. But is there any such thing as reincarnation as a law of nature, like gravity and other laws of nature? My answer is no. It doesn't matter whether you believe or not in reincarnation. If one is interested in finding out for himself and by himself, to resolve this problem of reincarnation, and get an answer for this oft-repeated question, "Is there such a thing as reincarnation?" you have to ask this fundamental question, "What is there now that you think will reincarnate?" Is there anything there? Is there any such thing as soul? Is there any such thing as the 'I'? Is there any such thing as the psyche? Whatever you see there, whatever you experience there is created only by the knowledge you have of that self. If you are lucky enough to be freed from the totality of knowledge, the knowledge of the self, reincarnation, and all kinds of things, then is it possible for you to experience any centre, any 'I', any self, any soul? So, to me the 'I' is nothing but a first person singular pronoun, and I do not see any centre or self there. So the whole idea of reincarnation is built only on the foundation of our beliefs.

Q : What is it that makes one a great person in due course of time and another stationary, stagnant in his mental processes? Do you attribute this to some kind of inherent gift?

U.G.: We have always been curious and interested in finding out why a child is born with deformities. And reincarnation was a very interesting theory evolved by the human mind at one time to explain *away* such situations and give us comfort in facing the situation that we have such people in our midst. But now it is possible for us, in the light of what they are doing in terms of genetic research and microbiology, to correct the deformities created by nature. Why should we want to attribute this misfortune to something terrible that we did in our previous life? That kind of belief comes in very handy to us. We have in our midst today a tremendous suffering, a tremendous amount of poverty, starvation, and degradation. It is very comforting for us to believe that, that suffering is there because the people who suffer did something terrible in their past life. That is no answer to give. That makes us take shelter in the belief and not do anything to solve the problem. The belief is neither spiritual nor human. In the name of doing something human to our fellow beings, we perpetrated inhuman deeds. The belief in reincarnation will only help us to look the other side and not to deal with the problem that is demanding answers from every thinking man in the world today.

Q : J. Krishnamurti always emphasized one fact, that is, nobody requires a *guru*. In fact, you too, I understand, would not like to be a *guru* for anybody. According to you, what is the role of a *guru* who shows the way for the *shishya*?

U.G.: I think that it is the wrong word to use in these days for all those spiritual gurus we have in the market, selling shoddy pieces of goods, and exploring the gullibility and credulity of people. A guru is one who tells you to throw away all the crutches that you have been made to believe are essential for your survival. The true guru tell you, "Throw them away, and don't replace them with the fancy crutches or even computerized crutches. You can walk; and if you fall, you will rise and walk again." Such is the man whom we consider, or even tradition considers, being the real guru, and not those who are selling those shoddy pieces of goods in the market place today. It is a business; it has become a holy business for people. I am not condemning anything. But as long as you depend upon somebody for solving your problems, so long you remain helpless. And this helplessness is exploited by the people who actually do not have the answers to your problems, but they give you some sort of a comforter. People are satisfied with these comforters and fall for this kind of thing, instead of dealing with the problems by themselves and for themselves.

Q : The spiritualism of the East and the spiritualism of the West are gradually exchanging places today, and you have seen the results of both now. What is the panacea for the human misery, the deprivation, the kind of suffering everyone in this planet is facing? Everyone has got something they want, something always to seek, to run after.

U.G.: As we started this discussion we said that the quest for happiness is all that anybody, whether he is a Russian, an American, an African, or an Indian, is interested in. I said that it is impossible to achieve such a goal because of the physical problem (of conflict with the body) that is involved in achieving that goal. It is assumed that the West is materialistic, and that it is looking towards the East for spiritual guidance. That is not really true. If you live for a longer period in the West, you will realize that those who are interested in these spiritual matters are not really the people who are guiding the destinies of this world. What is responsible for this sudden interest in spiritual matters and their looking to the East for succour is drugs. They gave them a new sort of experience. But they were not satisfied with repeating those experiences. They were looking around for varieties of religious experiences, whether they are from India, or from Japan or from China. They are attracted to these things because of the new language and new techniques.

The fact of the matter is that when once you have everything that you can reasonably ask for in this world, when all the material needs are taken care of, naturally the question arises, "Is that all?" When once you pose that question "Is that all?" to yourself, you have created a tremendous market for this kind of business, the holy business. These people are exploiting the gullibility and credulity of the people, rather than helping them to resolve the basic problems, the human problems. It is not that simple. So we have to ask such questions over and over again. But all the questions we are asking are born out of the answers that we already have. It never occurs to us to ask why we keep asking the questions when we already have the answers given by the sages, saints, and saviours of mankind. We fail to realize that the answers that they have given us are the ones that are responsible for the tragedy of mankind. We don't question them. If we question the answers, we would be questioning the teachers. If humanity is to be saved from the chaos of its own making, it has to be freed from the saviours of mankind. That does not mean that you should destroy everything. You will have to ask questions not born out of the answers we already have. But is there any answer? That is all. There it stops. And the solution is there for mankind.

The Robot is Dreaming

To be an individual and to be yourself, you do not have to do a thing. Culture demands that you should be something other than what you are. What a tremendous amount of energy we waste trying to become that! But if that energy is released, living becomes very simple. Then what is it that you cannot do?

Q: You mentioned that you could not bring back the experience of what happened when you were with Ramana Maharshi. But the brain science tells us that the brain records every experience in our life. Is it all there somewhere in the basement of the brain? How would you explain that?

U.G.: What I am trying to put across to those who are interested in listening to what I have to say is that there is no such thing as the totality of experiences. Memory is in frames. In order to explain what I mean when I say that it is all in frames and that the whole human body is functioning from moment to moment, it is necessary for us to understand one basic thing, that is, how the senses are operating. What is there is only a response to a stimulus. The response is not translated by anything that is there, except that it registers the stimuli in the same way as information is registered when transferring images from one floppy disc to another. There is no linking up of all these responses. Each one is an independent frame. A lot of imagination is involved in our trying to understand what actually is happening there.

I will give you the example of what a friend wanted me to do when I was in a hill resort in India. He said that when he reached the top of a particular mountain then he would have a 360-degree view of the whole place. So he dragged me up to the top. Unwillingly, hesitantly, I pushed myself to the top of that hill and tried to experience what he called a 360-degree view of the whole place. I said to myself, "That fellow is kidding himself and imagining things. How is it possible to experience the 360-degree view of this place? I can see only 180 degrees. So what he thinks he is experiencing is born out of his own imagination". This [*pointing to himself*] is singularly incapable of creating images. Translating the sensory perceptions into images is the cultural input here. When my eyes are not looking at you, there is no way that this organism [*pointing to himself*] can create the image of what you look like. The problem is the creation of images which is born out of our imagination and mostly out of what is put in there by our culture.

Q: I am listening...

U.G.: So what I am trying to say is that what the brain does is to translate these sensory perceptions into the framework of memory. Memory is not a constant factor. What happens is that when the light falls on the object and activates your optic nerve, it throws an image on the retina. This is what we have learnt from the study of our biology, and that is what the physiologists have taught us in our schools. But if you want to experience the fact, that is, the image of what you are looking at, it is something that cannot be experienced by us. Why I give this example is to free us from many of the ideas we have of what memory is. When once optic nerves are activated, they in turn activate the neurons in the brain, bring the memory into operation, and tell us that the object is this or that. So the next frame is quite different from the previous frame.

Let me give the example of movie camera. The movie camera captures whatever is happening in frames. You take, for example, the movement of my hand from here to there – it has ten different frames to show that the hand has moved from here to there. And in order to see the movement on the screen, you have to use an artificial thing called the projector. And only then do you see the movement of hand artificially created through the help of the projector. The sound is something like what they do in movie industry. The sound is nineteen and a half frames behind the corresponding picture frame. There is a gap between the picture you take and the sound – nineteen and a half frames. In exactly the same way, thought is very slow. By the time it comes and captures this "whatever is there" within its framework, your eyes have moved somewhere else, and that other thing is completely wiped out.

Q: I am thinking of television. It might be a good example too. There the picture is never really there. It is just a collection of dots. It requires the brain to put the picture together.

U.G.: The brain is operating in exactly the same way. The whole thing is registered as dots and the pictures are taken in frames. There is an illusion that there is somebody who is looking at the things. Actually there is nobody who is looking at the things. It may sound very strange to you when I say that there is nobody who is talking. You are the one that is making me talk; there is nobody here [*pointing to himself*] who is talking. There is nobody. It may sound very strange to you but that is the way it is. It is so mechanical, yet we are not ready to accept the mechanical functioning of this living organism.

Q: So, you have no sense of identity, personal identity, of yourself?

U.G.: No way, because there is no centre there; there is no psyche there; there is no 'I' there. The only 'I' that I can find there is the first person singular pronoun. I have to use that first person singular pronoun to differentiate it from the second person singular pronoun. That is all. But there is nothing there, which you can say is 'I'. That is the reason why I cannot tell myself that I am a free man, that I am an enlightened man, that you are not a free man. There is no need for me to free you or enlighten you because to do that I must have an image of myself and in relationship to that I can have an image of you. So, the images we have there are related to what we would like to be, what we ought to be, what we should be, and what we must be.

Q: As you travel around the world there are people that gather around you. Why do people gather around you, why do they come to see you?

U.G.: They still think that I can help them. I will relate to you some conversation that took place recently in Bangalore. They are all my friends. I don't have any devotees or disciples or · followers. I tell them that they are my followers because they are repeating whatever I am saying. And there is no use kidding themselves that they are not following me. The moment they repeat something, which is not theirs, they have become the followers of somebody.

On one occasion, when I asserted with great vehemence that whatever happened to me had happened despite everything, despite my visit to Ramana Maharshi, despite my contact with J. Krishnamurti and my personal conversations with him, and despite all the things that were expected of somebody who wanted to be an enlightened man, one friend in the audience said, "We cannot accept your statement of 'despite...'". He said that my statements were irrelevant. "The problem is very simple", he said, "If we accept what you are saying, namely, that whatever that happened to you has happened regardless of what you did, and that everything you did was irrelevant, we lose the only hope that we have in you. We still feel that although we have lost faith in them all, we cannot lose faith in you". I told him that that is the one thing that is standing there in him which makes it impossible for him to free himself from whatever he is trying to free himself from, because he has replaced one thing with another. That is all that we can do. One illusion is replaced by another illusion and one teacher is replaced by another teacher. There is no way you can function without replacing one thing with another.

Q: J. Krishnamurti maintained that there is no authority, no teacher, and that there is no path. Everyone has a life-path that has taken him to wherever he ought to be. You also have a life-path that has gotten you to where you are.

U.G.: But I cannot suggest anything that did not play a part in my life. That would be something false, falsifying the thing you see.

Q: Why should you not say that each of us has an individual and unique life-path and out of that comes whatever that is?

U.G.: The uniqueness of every individual cannot express itself because of the stranglehold of the experiences of others. After all, you don't exist, and I don't exist. You and I have been created by the totality of those experiences, and we have to use them in order to function sanely and intelligently in this world.

Q: So you are creating me now?

U.G.: You are creating me now.

Q: You are creating me now?

U.G.: No, I am not creating you because I don't have an image of myself here. So, whatever you see here [*pointing to himself*] is your creation and the projection of the knowledge you have of me. I don't know if you get what I am trying to say. I am not involved in what is going on there in you. What is involved here is only a reflection of whatever is there in front of me on the retina. But the translation of it is absent because it is part of that movement that is going on there.

Q: So, what I get from what you say is that it is a matter of living each moment as it comes.

U.G.: Such statements are very misleading. We place ourselves in a situation where we think that it is possible for us to live from moment to moment. But it is the body that is functioning from moment to moment.

Q: O.K. the body is functioning from moment to moment.

U.G.: The one that is interested in living from moment to moment, which is the mind (quote and unquote), cannot live that way because its survival depends upon repeated experiences. The continuity of the knowledge that it is 'me' is not something else.

You have to maintain that centre all the time, and the only way you can maintain that centre is through the repetitive process, repeating the same old experiences over and over again, and yet imagining that one day you are going to function from moment to moment. It is this hope that gives you the feeling and also some sort of experience that you are living from moment to moment. But the possibility of actually living from moment to moment is never there because the mind's interest is only to continue. Therefore, it has invented the idea of living from moment to moment, no-mind, and all that kind of stuff. Through these gimmicks it knows it can maintain its own continuity.

Q: Sometimes we are so involved with our activity that we lose ourselves in it, and in that sense we are living in the moment.

U.G.: It is not correct to say that, because your involvement in whatever you are doing is a sort of 'high'. It is an experience that you want to place on a higher level and then think that you are absorbed in it.

Q: But you are not thinking about it, for there is no interval.

U.G.: No, thought is very much there. But you have made that into an extraordinary experience, and your wanting to be like that always is one thing that is not possible. A musician thinks that he is absorbed in what he is doing. It is demanding your total attention to express whatever you are doing, and when two things are not there it is a lot easier for you to express it effectively than when you are thinking about it.

Q: I really think about experiences after they happen. Then I reflect on them. When I look up in the sky and see a

hawk flying across the sky, I see the hawk and afterwards I reflect on it, "Oh, I saw a hawk"! But at the moment when I see it I am not thinking about it.

U.G.: You see, that is not correct, because we have been made to believe, and you probably accept that statement, that while you are experiencing a thing you are not aware of it. The fact that you recall, whether you name that as a hawk or not, implies that you were very much there. I know a lot of people who tell me that they were in a thoughtless state, that there were moments when the 'I' was not there. But when once such a thing really happens, it is finished once and for all, and there is no way you can link those moments up together and create a continuity there. So, the statement that when you are experiencing a thing you are not aware of the experience and you become aware or conscious only after the experience is gone is highly questionable. If that were so, it would have shattered the whole experiencing structure once and for all. It would be something of an earthquake hitting this place, and what happens then nobody knows. A shifting of things would have taken place, and thereafter the organism functions in a very normal and natural way. It would have found a new sort of equilibrium.

Q: Why are we here as human beings, living right now?

U.G.: Why do we ask that question, "Why are we here?" What is it that tells you that you are here? Are you there now? It is the knowledge that tells you that you are here, that I am here.

Q: I have some awareness of being here, a feeling of being here.

U.G.: Feeling is also thought. We want to feel that feelings are more important than thoughts, but there is no way you can experience a feeling without translating that within the framework of the knowledge that you have. Take for example that you tell yourself that you are happy. You don't even know that the sensation that is there is happiness. But you capture that sensation within the framework of the knowledge you have of what you call a state of happiness, and the other state, that of unhappiness. What I am trying to say is that it is the knowledge that you have about yourself which has created the self there and helps you to experience yourself as an entity there.

I am not particularly fond of the word 'awareness'. It is misused. It is a rubbed coin, and everybody uses it to justify some of his actions, instead of admitting that he did something wrong. Sometimes you say, "I was not aware of what was going on there". But awareness is an integral part of the activity of this human organism. This activity is not only specifically in the human organism but also in all form of life – the pig and the dog. The cat just looks at you, and is in a state of choiceless awareness. To turn that awareness into an instrument which you can use to bring about a change is to falsify that. Awareness is an integral part of the activity of the living organism. And so, 'awareness' is not just the right kind of word to use.

It is impossible for us to separate ourselves from the rest of the things that are out there. You are not different from the chair that you are sitting on. But what separates you from the chair is the knowledge you have of that – "This is a chair", "You are sitting on the chair". But the fact is that the sensation that is involved in this relationship between you and the chair is the sense of touch. The sense of touch does not, however, tell you that you are separate from this chair on which you are sitting. I am not trying to say that you are the chair. That is too absurd.

Actually what makes you feel that the body is there is the gravitational pull of the body, the heaviness of the body. You feel the existence of the body because of the gravitational pull. I said somewhere in the beginning that you are affecting everything there and everything that is there is affecting you. The fact of this statement is something that cannot be experienced by you because it is one unitary movement. The moment you separate the two and say that this is the response to that, you have already brought the knowledge you have of the things into operation and told yourself that this is the response to that stimulus.

Q: The quantum physicists tell us that it is all connected and we are all part of the universe.

U.G.: But they have arrived at that as a concept. So did metaphysicians in India. They arrived at the fact and said that there is no such thing as space. Space is a very essential thing for you to survive in this world. But you can never experience the fact that there is such a thing as space. A scientist came to see me and made this statement that there is no such thing as time, and there is no such thing as matter. I said, "You are repeating a memorized statement. Probably you will give me an equation to prove that there is no such thing as space. But supposing it is a fact in your life that there is no space, (I always give crude examples,) what happens to your relationship with your wife?" When people throw these kinds of phrases to me – that there is no observer, or that the observer is the observed – I give them a hard time and try to make them realize the implications of what they are saying. It is very interesting for the theologians, the metaphysicians, and the scientists to discuss these things. But when it percolates to the level of our day-to-day existence, and of our relationships with the people around us, it is very different. If you tell yourself that the observer is the observed, and apply that to a situation where you are about to make love to your wife, what will happen?

Q: Is there a situation where the observer is really the observed?

U.G.: That is the end of all relationships. It's finished. To say the observer is the observed is a meaningless statement, repeated *ad nauseam*. They actually do not know what will happen when that is the case. All relationships will be finished.

Q: So we are just automata...

U.G.: Automatically repeating words and phrases, which are memorized. They have no relevance to the way we are functioning.

Q: Are you just an automation?

U.G.: Oh, I am an automation. There is no one thought which I can call my own. If this computer [*pointing to his head*] has no information on a particular subject, it is silent. So you are operating the computer [*pointing to himself*]. It is your interest to find out what is there in this computer. And whatever comes out of me is yours. What you call the printout is yours and you are reading something in it.

Q: So I am the dreamer and you are the dream.

U.G.: You have created me. You have all the answers and you are asking the questions.

Q: I think I already have answers.

U.G.: Otherwise how can there be questions? You are not sure that they are the answers.

Q: Well, I am like everyone here, asking questions that any person might ask.

U.G.: …for which they already have the answers. But they are not sure that they are the answers. And they don't have the guts to brush aside the persons that have given those answers. Sentiments come into picture there, and you lose the guts to throw away the answers, and the ones who have given the answers, out the window.

Q: What I get from this is that you have to be an individual.

U.G.: To be an individual and to be yourself you don't have to do a thing. Culture demands that you should be something other than what you are. What a tremendous amount of energy – the will, the effort – we waste trying to become that! If that energy is released, what is it that we can't do? How simple it would be for every one of us to live in this world! It is so simple.

A Jolt of Lightning

If there is anything like super consciousness or higher consciousness that people speak of, you are as much an expression of that as any of the claimants to that cosmic power. Every dog, every cat, every pig, every cow, the garden slug there, you, everybody, even Chengiz Khan and Hitler, and me are an expression of the same thing. Why should nature or some cosmic power, if there is one in the world, need the help of somebody as an instrument to express itself and help others?

Q: I think it was in 1967, just on your 49th birthday when you were listening to J. Krishnamurti's talk, it is said that an experience occurred to you. Would you describe that?

U.G.: I don't want to go into that in great detail. But what I have been emphasizing lately is that whatever has happened to me happened despite everything I did. Whatever I did or did not do, and whatever events people believed that led me into this [natural state] are totally irrelevant. It is very difficult for me to fix a point now and tell myself that this is me, and look back and try to find out the cause of whatever has happened to me, because this is not in the field of cause and effect relationship. That is why I emphasizing and overemphasizing all the time that it is acausal. That is very difficult for people to understand.

Q: By 'acausal' you mean that it happened without any preparations?

U.G.: That is what I am saying. It is something like, to use my favourite phrase, "Lighting hitting you, a jolt of lighting hitting you", and you don't know what you are left with. You have no way of finding out for yourself and by yourself what has happened to you. Has anything happened to me at all? But one thing I can say with certainty is that the very thing that I searched all my life was shattered to pieces. The goals that I had set for myself – self-realization, God-realization, transformation, radical or otherwise, or even enlightenment – were all false, and there was nothing there to be realized, and nothing to be found there. The very demand to be free from anything, even from the physical needs of the body, just disappeared, and I was left with nothing. Therefore, whatever comes out of me mow depends upon what you draw out of me.

I have actually and factually nothing to communicate, because there is no communication possible at any level. The only instrument we have is the intellect. We know, in a way, that this instrument has not helped us to understand anything. So, when once it dawns on you that this is not the instrument, and that there is no other instrument with which to understand anything, you are left with this puzzling situation that there is nothing to understand. In a way, it would be highly presumptuous on my part to sit on a platform or accept invitations like this and try to tell people that I have something to say, that I have come into something extraordinary, which nobody has come into.

But what I am left with *is* something extraordinary – extraordinary not in the sense that it has been possible for me through any effort or volition of mine, but in the sense that everything that every man thought, felt, and experienced before is thrown out of my system. So, you can say that it is, indeed, a courageous thing that has happened to me. But I cannot tell people that through courage you can put yourself into that kind of situation.

It is very difficult to tell people how it all happened to me. They are only interested in finding out how it happened to me, because their only interest is to find out the cause, find out what led me into this. But when I tell them that it is acausal, it is very difficult for them to understand and accept it. Their interest is to find out a cause and make it happen to them.

Q: I think it is useful sometimes to talk about one's realization in terms of when and what happened. In this context, going back to 1967, what happened to you when you were listening to J. Krishanamurti?

U.G.: You see when I was listening to him it suddenly dawned on me, "Why the hell have I been listening to this man? From this description I feel that I am in the same state as that man". I said to myself that I was in the same state as that man, assuming for the moment that he was in the same state that he was describing and in the same state that the great spiritual teachers were in. "What the hell have I been doing all my life? Why the hell am I sitting here listening to him?" I then walked out with just a single thought whirling in me, as it were, like in a whirlpool. "How do you know that you are in the same state?" I understand that the question implies that

I was familiar with the descriptions of various states. I had tried to simulate them in me and experience them, and that is all there is to it. So this question went on and on. But suddenly this question also disappeared. I said to myself that there is no reason for me to feel grateful to anybody, to express my thanks to anybody.

Whatever has happened to me has happened despite listening to this teacher or that teacher, or doing this, that, or the other. But if I say all this, it is something which is not very interesting to people. The want to *know*, and I tell them that I myself do not know. I cannot look at myself and tell myself that I am an enlightened man, that I am a free man, that tremendous changes have taken place in me. So, I use this phrase that we very often hear on the commercials. It is not something like "before and after wash"; no washing has helped me to reach anywhere. It is just a happening. I still have to use the word 'happening', because there is no other way that I can communicate this and give a feel of this to anybody else.

Q: It is all like an infant just coming into the world without any memory or thoughts, trying to see the world for the first time, and just figuring it out as to how it all works, just experiencing it. Will that be similar to what you are talking about?

U.G.: No, it is not correct to say that there is any kind of experience in newborn children, because we have no way of going through that all over again. Anything we simulate and try to experience is only from where we stand today. And where we stand today is the product of experiences of all kinds. So, anything we experience, although we call it rebirthing or trying to experience what it was like when we were a newborn baby or an infant, is naturally coloured by where we stand today. Anything we experience has no relevance, no meaning to what I am trying to say.

There are many people who talk of rebirthing. It has become fashionable for people to indulge in that kind of fantasy. You know in Japan they have some techniques in which by manipulating certain nerves at the base of your head they will make you go through the experience of your own birth. I have always maintained that the experiencing structure is totally absent at the time of our birth. And, I always questioned the psychologists, especially Freud, when he made the statement that birth is a traumatic experience, I don't think that it is a traumatic experience at all, because there is no experiencing structure there at all. Actually it is very difficult to say as to when the experiencing structure in babies comes into operation. I am one of those who believe that the influence of environment is very limited on us. (I maintain that I am not an authority on such things). But the experiencing structure is genetic in its origin and in its expression. Everything is genetically controlled. If we really want to change individuals, the only way we can do it is not by changing the environment, not through changing the cultural input, but by trying to understand what really is the part that genes play in us. Maybe through some kind of genetic engineering we can create perfect human beings.

Q: So, you would support genetic engineering?

U.G.: No, I do not. I am at the same time conscious of the fact that it is a very dangerous thing that we are indulging in. When once we perfect these engineering techniques, we will hand them over to the state. Thereafter it will be a lot easier for the state to manipulate individuals and turn them into mere robots. (I am not against robots, as we are actually robots, whether we like it or not). The state will make people do things, which they are unwilling to do. Usually it takes a lot of time and a lot of brainwashing to teach something to people – to make people believe in God, to make people believe in a particular political ideology. Conversely, to free them from some kind of belief we have to brainwash them all over again. It is a very elaborate and long process. But it is a lot easier and faster for us to use these techniques of genetic engineering to change individuals than it is possible otherwise.

Q: You know we were speaking about J. Krishnamurti. He claims to have no memory of this process. It is the same thing that has happened to you? Do you have a memory?

U.G.: I don't want to say anything about Krishnamurti. I don't have any idea of what happened to him. I don't know what he meant when he said this. Actually your memory becomes extraordinary after this happening. But the problem that we have to face today is different. We have been using our memory a lot. I always maintain (you may question this, and the experts in the field of brain psychology may question it; but one of these days they will have to accept what I am trying to say) that the brain plays a very minor role in the functioning of the body. It is not a creator at all. It is just a reactor. What this memory is we really don't know yet. One of these days the experts who are dealing with this problem of memory will have to come out with answers to questions like what these neurons are.

I maintain that memory is not located in any particular area of the body. Every cell in our body is involved. And my feeling is that we have come to a point in the history of mankind where we have to confront the problem of people who have lost their memories. We have put our memory and our brain to such use for which they are not intended. This is one of the reasons why we find that Alzheimer's disease, or whatever you want to call it, is on the increase. The other day I heard that one in two of those in the eighty-year-old bracket are affected by it. You know recently there was also a report of the same disease in England. Six hundred thousand people are affected by this problem there.

Q: You mentioned about the misuse of brain.

U.G.: Misusing memory. Using memory for purpose for which it is not intended. After all, what are you? You are a memory. We have to use memory in order to survive in the world created by our society, culture, or whatever you want to call it. There is no other way. I know that it is an extension of the same survival mechanism. No doubt it is.

Q: When you burn your finger you withdraw it at once.

U.G.: Automatically. There you don't have to use your memory. That is the way this human body is functioning. But to survive in this world that we have created, our world of culture, society, or whatever you want to call it, the constant use of memory is essential. The whole of our education is built on the foundation of how to develop our memory. I am afraid that I am going off on a tangent.

Q: Yes.

U.G.: I usually hop, jump, and skip. Let me try to stick to this point, which I am trying to make. Unfortunately, humanity has placed before itself the model of a perfect man. The idea of the perfect man is born out of the value system that we have created. That value system is born out of the behaviour patterns of the great teachers of mankind.

Q: Jesus might be an example of …

U.G.: Jesus, Buddha, and all the great teachers. Every human body, however, is unique. Nature is not interested in creating a perfect being. Its interest is to create only a perfect species.

Q: If every one of us is unique, that implies that our code of enlightenment, if there is such a thing, would also be unique so that each of us reaches that state individually and uniquely.

U.G.: Exactly. That is what I am trying to emphasize. It is just not possible for us to produce enlightened people on an assembly line. You know, if look at history, even a country like India which prides itself as a land of spirituality has produced only a very few enlightened people. You can count them on your fingers. But unfortunately, in the market place, we have many claimants who say that are enlightened, and they are in turn out to enlighten everybody. There is a market for that kind of thing. The demand and supply principal is responsible for that. But actually an enlightened man or a free man, if there is one, is not interested in freeing and enlightening anybody. This is because he has no way of knowing that he is a free man, that he is an enlightened man. It is not something that can be shared with somebody, because it is not in the area of experience at all.

There is no such thing as a new experience. Suppose you go to a new place. What goes on in your mind, if I may use the word, is that you are always trying to fit whatever you are seeing into the framework of the past. The moment you say that something is new, it is the old that is telling you that it is new. So, it is very difficult for us to experience anything new because, if there is something really new, it is not in particular frames that the old is destroyed, but the totality of the past is destroyed in one great big blow.

Q: In effect what you are saying is that we cannot experience anything new.

U.G.: Yes. You may not agree with me, but brush this aside as absurd and nonsense. But there is no such thing as a new experience. There is nothing new at all. It is the old that tells us that it is new, and through this gimmick thought is making what it calls new part of the old, and is thus maintaining its continuity. So, whatever you cannot experience does not exist. It may sound very dogmatic assertion on my part, but when you try to experience something that you have not experienced before, the whole movement of the experiencing structure comes to an end.

Q: Having read some accounts of previous life, I go back to the experience that you had when you went to see Ramana Maharshi. You asked him, "Whatever it is you have, can you give it to me?" And he said, "I can give it, but can you take it?"

U.G.: Unfortunately, that is the traditional answer that is dished out by all the spiritual teachers. What is reported in the so-called story of my life is a garbled version of what I actually felt at that time. Anyway, anything I say today is irrelevant, because I don't know what I felt at that particular moment, and there is no way I can relive that experience from here, I said to myself. "What is it that he has? If there is anybody in this world who can receive it, it is I". I said this to myself and walked out. That, in a way, decided another phase of my life.

The old traditional approach to the whole question of enlightenment was thrown out of my system, although I continued to read books on religion, studied philosophy, psychology, and science. I tried to find out answers from those people who have not been contaminated by the traditional teachings. I got interested in Western philosophy and science, and tried to find out the answer to my basic question. My basic question was one question: "Where is this mind that we are so concerned about, that we are trying to understand, study, and change? Why do we talk of a total change in the makeup of the mind? I don't see any such thing as mind

there at all, let alone a transformation or mutation of the mind".
This question always intrigued me and I questioned everybody
about the mind. I tried to get answers from every area of human
thought, but nothing helped me to find out the answers to those
questions. At that time I didn't have the certainty that I have today.
The certainty I have today that there is no mind is something which
I cannot transmit to anybody, however hard I may try, because
the very thing which we are using to communicate is in jeopardy,
and you are not ready to accept that possibility.

Q: The Buddhists also talk about no mind.

U.G.: They made a tremendous structure out of that
philosophical thought. They talked of the void. They talked of
emptiness. You know the whole Buddhist philosophy is built on
the foundation of that "no mind". Yet they have created tremendous
techniques of freeing themselves from the mind. All the Zen
techniques of meditation try to free you from the mind. The very
instrument that we are using to free ourselves from the thing called
"mind" is the mind. Mind is nothing other than what you are doing
to free yourself from the mind. But when it once it dawns on you,
by some strange chance or miracle, that the instrument that you
are using to understand everything is not the instrument, and that
there is no other instrument, it hits you like a jolt of lighting.

Love is Only a Trump Card

When everything fails, you use the last card, the
trump in the pack of cards, and call it love.

**Q: When man is the same everywhere why is there so
much difference among men? I find a contradiction between
the problems that man is facing in America and Europe and
those he is facing in underdeveloped countries. For example,
drugs, sex, crime, and pleasure are the issues in America
and West European countries, but poverty, lack of education,
and death due to malnutrition are the issues in the
underdeveloped countries.**

U.G.: The difference is artificially created by the Western
nations. They had the advantage of the technical know-how, which
was born out of the industrial revolution. When the revolution
went to America, with the help of that technical know-how they
exploited the resources of God's plenty there. You know there
was a time when anybody could go to the United States without a
passport. But in 1911 they introduced the necessity to have a

passport to enter the United States. In 1923 they introduced the immigration laws. Once you are there in a particular place and establish yourself and your rights, it is finished. (I am giving this as an example, but this applies to every country.) If anybody lands and colonizes any place on any planet, they will establish their rights there and prevent all other nations from landing there. The Americans established these same rights. It was God's plenty that helped the nations to develop and hold on to what they have. But they continue to exploit the resources of the rest of the worlds as well as their own resources. Even today they are doing that. They don't want to give up.

Basically, human nature is exactly the same whether in India or in Russia or in America or in Africa. Human problems are exactly the same. All the problems are artificially created by the various structures created by human thinking. As I said, there is some sort of (I can't make a definitive statement) neurological problem in the human body. Human thinking is born out of this neurological defect in the human species. Anything that is born out of human thinking is destructive. Thought is destructive. Thought is a protective mechanism. It draws frontiers around itself, and it wants to protect itself. It is for the same reason that we also draw lines on this planet and extend them as far as we can. Do you think these frontiers are going to disappear? They are not. Those who have entrenched themselves, those who have had the monopoly of all the world's resources so far and for so long, if they are threatened to be dislodged, what they would do is anybody's guess. All the destructive weapons that we have today are here only to protect that monopoly.

But I am sure that the day has come for people to realize that all the weapons that we have built so far are redundant and that they cannot be used any more. We have arrived at a point where you cannot destroy your adversary without destroying yourself.

So it is that kind of terror, and not the love and brotherhood that has been preached for centuries, that will help us to live together. But this has to percolate to the level of human consciousness. (I don't want to use the word 'consciousness' or 'human consciousness' because there is no such thing as consciousness at all. I use that word only for purpose of communication.) Until this percolates to the level of human consciousness, in the sense that man sees that he cannot destroy his neighbour without destroying himself. I don't think it will help. I am sure that we have come to that point. Whenever and wherever you have an edge over your adversary or your neighbour, you will still continue to exercise what you have been holding on to for centuries. So, how are you going to solve the problem? All utopias have failed.

The whole mischief originated in the religious thinking of man. Now there is no use in blaming the religious thinking of man, because all the political ideologies, even your legal structures, are the warty outgrowth of the religious thinking of man. It is not so easy to flush out the whole series of experiences which have been accumulated through centuries, and which are based upon the religious thinking of man. There is a tendency to replace one belief with another belief, one illusion with another illusion. That is all we can do.

Q: The developed nations know fully well that if there is a war today they will face total annihilation. There will be no victor left anywhere. But still there are these skirmishes here and there, and there is so much violence everywhere. Why is it so? Is it because that human nature, as some people say, is basically violent?

U.G.: Yes it is. Because thought is violent, anything that is born out of thought is destructive. You may cover it up with all wonderful and romantic phrases: "Love thy neighbour as thyself". Don't forget that in the name of "Love thy neighbour as thyself" millions and millions of people have died, more than in all the recent wars put together. But we now have come to a point where we can realize that violence is not the answer, that it is not the way to solve human problems. So, terror seems to be the only way. I am not talking of terrorists blowing up churches, temples, and all that kind of thing, but the terror that if you try to destroy your neighbour you will possibly destroy yourself. That realization has to come down to the level of the common man.

This is the way the human organism is functioning too. Every cell is interested in its own survival. It knows in some way that its survival depends upon the survival of the cell that is next to it. It is for this reason that there is a sort of cooperation between the cells. That is how the whole organism can survive. It is not interested in utopias. It is not interested in your wonderful religious ideas. It is not interested in peace, bliss, beatitude, or anything. Its only interest is to survive. That is all it is interested in. the survival of a cell depends upon the survival of the cell next to it. And your survival and my survival depend upon the survival of our neighbour.

Q: Whatever you say, I feel that the only way for humanity to survive is to bring about a change in the heart– and that is Love.

U.G.: No, not at all, because love implies division, separation. As long as there is division, as long as there is separation within you, so long do you maintain that separation around you. When everything fails, you use the last card, the trump in the pack of cards, and call it Love. But it not going to help us, and it has not helped us at all. Even religion has failed to free man from violence and from ten other different things that it is trying to free us from. You see it is not a question of trying to find new concepts, new ideas, new thoughts, and new beliefs.

As I said before, what kind of human being do you want on this globe? The human being modelled after the perfect being has totally failed. The model has not touched anything there. Your value system is the one that is responsible for the human malady, the human tragedy, forcing everybody to fit into that model. So, what do we do? You cannot do anything by destroying the value system, because you replace one value system with another. Even those who rebelled against religion, like those in the Communist countries, have themselves created another kind of value system. So, revolution does not mean the end of anything. It is only a revolution of our value system. So, that needs another revolution, and so on and so on. There is no way.

The basic question that we all have to ask for ourselves is, what kind of a human being you want? The only answer to this human problem, if there is any answer, is not to be found through new ideas, new concepts, or new ideologies, but through bringing about a change in the chemistry of the human body. But there is a danger even there. When once we perfect genetic engineering and change the human being, there will be a tendency to hand this technology over to the state. It will then be a lot easier for them to push all the people into war and see that can kill without a second thought. You don't have to brainwash them. You don't have to teach them love or patriotism. Brainwashing takes a century, as brainwashing to believe in God took centuries. The Communists took decades to brainwash their people not to believe in God. But with genetic engineering, there is no need for that kind of brainwashing process. It is a lot easier to change human beings by giving just one injection.

Q: What is being said in the Western world is that people there are very happy and perfectly satisfied with the changes taking place: there is the rule of law, respect for human

rights, free market economy, freedom of expression and speech, etc.

U.G.: Do you really think that there is freedom in the United States? What does that mean to a starving man – freedom of speech, freedom of worship, and freedom of the press? He does not know how to read the newspapers and is not interested in them. At least in the Communist systems they fed, clothed, and sheltered people, though that is now being denied to them in those nations. There is more unemployment than ever before in the Western countries. I don't think this is the model for the whole of mankind.

The whole system depends upon the exploitation of the resources of the world for the benefit of the Western nations. These laws that you are talking about are always backed by force. You know as a lawyer that the decision handed down by a judge is always backed by force. Ultimately, it is the force that counts. We all agree to submit ourselves to the decision of the judge. If you don't want to submit to them, the only recourse you have is to use violence. So all the gangsters get together and create a legal structure that is favourable to them. That they enforce on others through the help of violence, through the help of force.

What right do you have to create this blockade, for example, today around Iraq? What is the international law, which these people are talking about? I want to know. You as a lawyer know. What happened when America attacked and occupied Granada, a small nation? Nobody ever objected to it; nobody ever created a blockade there. I am not impressed by the international law and its legal structure. As long as it is advantageous to you, you talk of law. When the law fails you use force. Don't you?

Q: May I return to the question of certain other institutions of the human beings?

U.G.: You are a lawyer and the law is there probably to maintain the status quo. Is it not? So you cannot talk against the status quo.

Q: May I tell you that there are different schools of thought in the legal field?

U.G.: That is only a theological discussion. You know what all the theologians indulge in – God is this, God is that, the Ontological, the Teleological and the Cosmological arguments for the existence of God. All these different schools of law you are referring to are no different from the discussions of the theologians.

Q: What do you think of the institution of marriage and family?

U.G.: The institution of marriage is not going to disappear. As long as we demand relationships, it will continue in some form or other. Basically, it is a question of possessiveness. There was a time when I believed that economic independence for women would solve many of the problems in India. But when I visited America I was shockingly surprised that even those women who are economically independent wanted to possess their drunkard husbands. The husband was beating her everyday, and twice on Sundays. I know many cases. I am not generalizing, but possessiveness is the most important element. The basis of relationships is: "What do I get out of the relationship?" That is the basis of all human relationships. As long as I can get what I want the relationships last.

The marriage institution will somehow continue because it is not just the relationship between the two, but children and property are involved. So it is not going to disappear overnight at all. And we use property and children as a pretext to give continuity to the institution of marriage. The problem is so complex and so complicated. It is not so easy for anybody to come up with answers to the age-old institution of marriage.

I can tell you one thing. A lot of couples come to see me with their problems. Unmarried, unwed couples, if you listen to their stories, you cannot imagine their miseries. And yet they cannot part company.

Unmarried couples are more miserable than married couples. The answer is not so easy. As long as we want to establish a relationship, so long this institution will remain. Maybe it will be modified, changed to suit the changing condition.

A leader of the feminist movement (I am a crude and brutal man) came to see me. She asked me, "What do you think of the feminist movement?" I said, "I am on your side; by all means fight for your rights. But remember that as long as you depend on a man for your sexual needs, so long you are not free. The other way round is also true: if you can satisfy your sexual needs with the help of a vibrator – that is a different matter. But if you want a man to satisfy you sexual needs, you are not free.

Q: You say that the family is not a solution, unwed relations are not a solution. What other institutions do you have in mind?

U.G.: It is these institutions, which are responsible for the misery of mankind. There is no way you can change or modify these institutions. It is a lot easier for people in India now to go for a divorce than it was in earlier times. There was no question of me divorcing my wife or my wife divorcing me at that time. Now it is a lot easier. The changing conditions are responsible for a change in our ideas. But that does not mean that the problem has an easy and simple solution.

Q: Will there not be anarchy if you do not support the male and female relationship and the family?

U.G.: If they are ready to accept the misery [*laughs*], it is well and good. But it is a miserable situation. They are not happy with that. Total anarchy is a state of being rather than a state of doing. There is no action in total anarchy. It is a state of being. So why are we frightened of anarchy? The anarchy that you are talking about is the destruction of the institutions, which we have built with tremendous care, and of our belief that those institutions should continue forever. So, it is that we are fighting for – to preserve them in their pristine purity.

Q: Are you not worried about the prospect of old age and the future of children when there is no family?

U.G.: It is society that has to take care of that problem. Why are you all paying taxes to the government if they don't do what they are supposed to do? It is the responsibility of each individual that he should do what he has promised to do. The problem is that once you put these individuals in the seat of power, then there is less chance of their sharing their power with others. And you provide them with tremendous weapons of destruction. A man like me who expresses this view will become the enemy of the state. They will not hesitate to destroy me. I don't care if I am destroyed. If they say, "Don't talk", I will stop talking. I don't believe in freedom of speech at all. If they say, "Don't talk", "what you are saying is a threat to mankind and to its institutions", "Good bye". I don't want to talk. I am not interested in changing the world. But they have promised to do certain things. You have elected them to the office; you have put them there in the seat of power and have unfortunately provided them with the most destructive of weapons. They will not hesitate to use them against you and me.

But these days there is no way you can use your nuclear weapons. I often say that if Bhutan invades India, India has no way of protecting itself. Bhutan is not going to invade India, unless it has the backing of some powerful nations. So, we are puppets of these people. We are spending so much money on defence. Defence against what? We talk of freedom of speech. If they say, "Don't talk", I am not interested in talking. I am not interested in saving individuals. And I am not interested in saving mankind.

Q: You spoke about the state's collecting taxes and said that the state should do everything to give security to the people and their children.

U.G.: I do not see any reason why anybody should starve on this planet. What are you doing to solve these problems? You may very well throw that same question at me. But I have not set myself up in the business of running this world. *They* have set themselves up in the business of ruling this or that country. What justification do you have for the fact that forty percent of the people are allowed to starve in India today? It is not spiritual; it is not human either. It is inhuman to let your fellow beings starve. Religion has invented that wonderful thing called charity. Not only that; you don't stop there, but you give the Nobel Prize to somebody because of the charitable work that particular individual is doing. That is the most vicious and vulgar thing that the religious man has come up with today.

Every one has a right to be fed. Nature has provided us with a bounty. But we are individually responsible for the inequities of this world. Don't ask me. " What are you doing about that?" I am not here running a crusade against these people. You have set your self up to solve these problems. If you don't solve them, something is wrong not with the leaders but with the people who have put them there in the seat of power. If they don't do what they are expected to do, change those rogues. I have no business to tell someone how to run these governments; I am not running these governments at all. What business do I have to tell them that this is the way you should run the government. It is the responsibility of everybody to contribute his mite, his share. But the world remains exactly the way it has been forever. Nobody wants any change.

Q: But you said that the state should do a number of things for the people.

U.G.: First thing, the state has to feed, clothe, and shelter everybody.

Q: Why is it that there is a maximum number of suicides and a maximum number of Aids cases even in countries like Switzerland where there is so much prosperity and high national income?

U.G.: That is a different problem. What do you mean by 'Aids'? Not the disease Aids?

Q: Yes, the disease Aids.

U.G.: That is the mistake we have made. One of the experiments went wrong. It is easy for us to blame the homosexuals, but the source of it is somewhere else. Did you read it in the paper? I think it is there in the paper: that the Nizam's wife died of Aids in India: yes, it is there in that Society Magazine. He admitted finally that his wife died of Aids. Who is responsible for that I do not know. Somebody says it is a transfusion of blood that caused it. I don't know. I haven't read that article. I am very frivolous in expressing my opinions. It doesn't matter. I am as well informed as anybody else in this world. I have seen the world.

We are Heading Towards Disaster

If those who have had the monopoly of all the worlds' resources so far and for so long are threatened to be dislodged, what they would do is anybody's guess. All the destructive weapons that we have today are only to protect them.

Q: What are your views regarding those who want to understand what this life is all about?

U.G.: The demand to understand and bring about the change in you is the one that is responsible for the demand to understand the world and then bring about a change in the world. They are one and the same. That is why you are interested in listening to others. Through that listening you think you will be able to bring about a change in you and then also a change in the world around you. Basically there is no difference between what is here [*pointing towards himself*] and what is out there in the world. There is no way you can draw a line of demarcation.

One thing that I always emphasize is that it is culture that has created us all for the sole purpose of maintaining its status quo and its continuity. So in that sense I do not see that there are any individuals at all. At the same time, the same culture has given us the hope that there is something that you can do to become an individual and that there is such a thing as free will. Actually there is no free will at all.

The most important thing for us to realize is that thought is a very destructive weapon, and that it is our enemy. However, we are not ready to accept the fact that thought can only create problems, but cannot help us to solve them.

Q: People go to gurus and read religious texts to bring about a change in their lives. But you completely brush aside all that. Why?

U.G.: My point is that there is nothing there to be changed. What these gurus in the market place are doing is to sell you some ice packs and provide you with some comforters. But when you come to me, you find it very difficult for the simple reason that I do not offer you any solution to your problems. My interest is to point out that there are actually no problems, and what we are saddled with are only solutions. Also, we are not ready to accept the fact that the solutions that these people have been offering us for centuries are not really the solutions. If they were really the solutions, the problems would have been solved long ago. If they are not the solutions, and if there are no other solutions, then there are no problems to be solved.

Q: Sweeping changes are taking place all over Europe and the Soviet Union. What part can India play in the new scenario that is emerging all over the world? The gurus who have been going to the West preaching Yoga and a number

of other attractive new concepts can perhaps take advantage of the situation.

U.G.: The changes that are taking place in Russia are actually no good for Russia and no good for the world. What has happened in Russia is that they have found suddenly, or at least the leaders of the Soviet Union have, that their Communist system of government has failed. But instead of finding solutions for their problems within the framework, they are looking for them somewhere else. I do not think India has any answers for these problems, nor do the Western nations for that matter. The total failure of the Communist philosophy or ideology or system of government there in the Soviet Union has unfortunately created a void. I am afraid that the Russian Orthodox Church will take advantage of the situation and step in. If it stops there, there is not much of a danger. But all these cults that have thrived on the gullibility and credulity of people in the Western nations will make a beeline to Russia and exploit people there. That is one thing that the Russians should try to avoid. But there seems to be no way that this exploitation or the other things that foreign countries are exporting to that country can be avoided. I do not see an adequate reason why America should export organically grown potato chips to Russia. Let me say one thing very clearly: it is not your democracy, freedom of speech, or freedom of a hundred and ten different things that these nations proclaim, that won Russia over to this side. It is the Coca-Cola in China and Pepsi Cola in Russia, and then also McDonald hamburgers. That is all that the Western nations can do there: they have created a market for people to step in and exploit.

This is what I tell even the scientists and psychologists who come to see me. In Fact, they also have come to the end of their tether. They are not able to tackle the problems that they are confronted with today – both in the field of psychology and in modern science. They have to find solutions only within the framework. Unfortunately they look towards Vedanta from India, to the religious answers that come from Japan or China. But actually those don't have any answers. If the greatest heritage of India cannot help India, how in the name of God do you think it will help other nations? I don't think India has any contribution to make to the world. This is what I strongly feel.

At least you see the West has high-tech and technology to offer to those countries. Through the help of this technology the West will probably do something to enrich those countries. Russia has tremendous natural resources still untapped – oil, gold, diamonds, and other things. High-tech and technology can help there. What can India offer to those nations? I don't see that India can offer anything. It is a total mess there. We can pat on our backs and feel that the great heritage of India has kept us going through the centuries. But we are in a sorry mess in India. If you say that this is only *my* opinion, it doesn't matter. I am not trying to win anybody over to my point of view. And nobody can win me over to his point of view. And there it stops.

Q: In spite of the radical changes that are taking place in the world, especially in Europe and Russia, I find that there is a revival of the old religion.

U.G.: The religious revivalism that you are talking about is there in the Western countries. There is this whole talk of "Back to Jesus", "Back to the Heritage of India", "Back to Islam", back to this, that, and the other. I am afraid that the rise of Islam not only in the Moslem world but also in Russia and China is going to be a formidable force. Once this cry of holy war, 'Jihad', spreads around, we will not know how to tackle that problem. I am not singing a doomsday song. That is what you are going to face very soon. Islam is going to be a formidable force in the world.

Q: I have been to the United States and Europe. I feel there is much jubilation and expectation in the minds of the politicians there that the world is changing for the better. But I find suddenly this crisis in the Middle East. What do you think about the future of the world in this context?

U.G.: I don't know. I am not a prophet. I cannot say anything, but like anybody else, I can hazard, if may use the word, a view of the shape of things to come. I don't know for sure, and nobody knows for that matter, what will happen.

There is one thing that I want to say, emphasize, and overemphasize, that there is no way we can reverse the whole thing. We are heading towards a disaster. Man must realize (and there seems to be no hope of his coming to terms with the reality of the situation) that thought, and all that is born out of our thinking, are the enemy of mankind, and there is nothing to replace that. Religious revivalism is not really the answer.

I personally feel that the basic question, which we all should ask ourselves is, what kind of human beings we want on this planet? Unfortunately, culture, whether it is Oriental or Occidental, has placed before us the model of a perfect being. That model is patterned after the behaviour of the religious thinkers of mankind who have done more harm than good. Everything that we are confronting today is a product of the religious thinking of man. But that thinking has no answers for the future of mankind. So if you want, you have to find answers within the framework of the systems that have failed to deliver the goods. I don't think religious thinking has any answers for our problems today.

The two things that we have to bear in mind are high-tech and technology. They will help us to solve the problems of this planet. Genetic engineering and the understanding of microbiology will take care of what kind of human beings you want. (They now say that we are genetically deficient and that the brain is neurologically deficient in many areas.)

Q: What about the problems of the underdeveloped countries, like poverty and lack of education?

U.G.: Do you mean to say that literacy is the solution or answer for the problems of India? We want to educate the people so that they can read our newspapers, and through the media you are going to brainwash these people. In India there are still peasants who are touched by the modern man. They are something unique. I don't know. I have never visited any village recently. But I really don't think educating people in the sense that we are talking about, the literacy we are talking about, is the way to really educate people. Let me give you the example of my grandmother. My grandmother was not a literate person, although she knew how to read and sign papers. I learned more from her about Advaita than I did from the professors at the University of Madras. She was not an educated woman. She knew all about the great culture of India. So, educating the masses to be literate is really not the answer. We have tremendous power of media at our disposal. If this power is in the hands of the government, there is nothing that *you* can do to avoid its influence. Also, if you take the example of the United States, their so-called free media are in no way better than the media that are under the grip of the government. Both are the same. I don't know, I am expressing a lot of opinions.

Q: I feel what you are saying is that the present technological and scientific changes are the only answers for this world.

U.G.: Yes, but I must say one thing. Whatever achievements we have had so far through the help of high-tech and technology have benefited only a limited number of people on this planet. If what they say is true, it is possible to feed twelve billion people with the resources at our command, the resources that nature has provided us, without the aid of high-tech and technology. But then why amongst five billion people is there poverty and misery? The answer is very simple. We are individually responsible for them, and it is not some curse of the high gods.

The rich nations are not going to give up their riches unless they are forced to give them up. You see, the nine rich nations, the nine industrial nations, sit here and dictate their terms. Are they going to give up the whole of the natural resources of the world? I don't think so, unless they are forced to. If they are forced to give them up, what they would do is anybody's guess. Even if they have everything to lose, I don't think they are going to give up anything.

Even this man sitting here who is a pacifist will fight to the end to protect his way of life and his way of thinking. I don't believe him at all. He will fight. He may be pacifist today, but tomorrow, if everything he has were to be taken away from him, I wouldn't be surprised if he were to kill me also, his best friend.

Q: You do not sound much of an optimist.

U.G.: What does it mean – the difference between an optimist and a pessimist? It is just a very clever way of putting things – that optimist does not give up and he still, somehow, has faith that he can maintain his own way of life and his own way of thinking. That is all. He would resort to any kind of force to maintain that way of life and that way of thinking.

Q: I feel that many things you have been talking about for the last few years are coming true.

U.G.: But I don't sit here patting myself on my back. And telling myself, or you, "I told you so". No, not at all.

The End of Illusion is Death

There is no such thing as death at all for this body. The only death is the end of the illusion, the end of the fear, the end of the knowledge, which we have about ourselves, and the world around us.

Q: In listening to you and reading your books I get the feeling that what you are saying is that there is no self, no soul, no anything whatsoever. What you are saying is that the whole of life lives in a physical form as experienced by the senses.

U.G.: Not separate from or independent of the life around us. It is one single unit. I cannot make any definitive statement, but somewhere along the line self-consciousness occurred in man which separated us from the totality of life around us. (We do not know for sure if there is any such thing as evolution; it is an assumption on our part. We accept what those who are in the know of things say. Those people have observed certain things and have established what they call a theory of evolution.)

Q: Do you mean to say that all the life that we experience is only through the body, through the senses, and that the body contains the whole human being?

U.G.: What exactly do you mean by "life"? Nobody knows anything about life, and there is no point in defining it. Anything that we say of life is a speculation on our part. What we are trying to understand or experience, life or whatever, is through the help of the knowledge we have of it. But thought is something dead. It is something that can never touch anything living. The moment it tries to touch life and capture it, contain it and give expression to it, it is destroyed by the living quality of life. What we mean by life, however, is not actually life but living. Living is our relationship with the people around us, the life around us, with the whole world around us. And that is all we know. That relationship is actually not a basic relationship, but one that is born out of our demand to become one with life. So anything we do, any attempt we make to become one with it, is fruitless because there is no way we can establish any relationship with the life around us.

Q: Why do you say that we are not part of it?

U.G.: I am not for a moment assuming or emphasizing that we are not part of it. We *are* part of it. But the most important question that we should ask ourselves is, "What is it that separates us from the life around us, and what is it that maintains the separateness, or division, if I may use the word, all the time?" Actually, what divides us is thought. Thought is matter. But that matter cannot stay there for long. The moment the matter is born it has to become part of the energy again. But this demand on our part, or on the part of thought, to maintain continuity, is the demand that drives us to experience the same thing over and over and over again. And thus we are maintaining this superficial, artificial, non-existent duality, division there between our life and the life around us.

Q: Thought is considered to be part of the brain. What could be the purpose of the brain? There seems to be a conflict between the body and the mind.

U.G.: It is only an assumption on our part, and I would say it is a false assumption, that thoughts are spontaneous and self-generated. They are not. Thought is only a response to stimuli. The brain is not really a creator; it is just a container. The function of the brain in this body is only to take care of the needs of the physical organism and to maintain its sensitivity, whereas thought, through its constant interference with sensory activity, is destroying the sensitivity of the body. That is where the conflict is. The conflict is between the need of the body to maintain its sensitivity and the demand of thought to translate every sensation within the framework of the sensual activity. I am not condemning sensual activity. Mind, or whatever word you want to call it, is born out of this sensuality. So all activities of the mind are sensual in their nature, whereas the activity of the body is to respond to the stimuli around it. That is really the basic conflict between what you call the mind and the body.

Q: So you say that the mind, the brain has really no nonphysical traces?

U.G.: I don't think there is any such thing as mind separate from the activity of the brain.

Q: Would you say that the brain has no nonphysical function?

U.G.: It is not interested in sensual activity. It is not interested in any experiences that the mind is interested in and is demanding. It is not even interested in the so-called spiritual experiences, the religious experiences like bliss, beatitude, immensity, and happiness.

Happiness is something that the body is not interested in. It cannot take it for long. Pleasure is one of the things that it is always rejecting. The body does not know, and does not even want to know, anything about happiness.

Q: Happiness is only a thinking quality, a sensual experience.

U.G.: Happiness is a cultural input there. Is there any such thing as happiness? I would say, no. So, the quest for happiness is a cultural input, and that is the common desire that we know exists everywhere, in every part of the world. That is what we all want, and that *want* is the most important want in human beings everywhere. Happiness, if you want to use the word, is like any other sensation. The moment thought separates itself from what is called the sensation of happiness, the demand to keep that sensation going longer than its natural duration also occurs with it. So, the body rejects any sensation, however extraordinary, however pleasant it may be. Keeping that sensation going longer than its duration of life is destroying the sensitivity of this living organism. That is the battle that is going on there. If you do not know what happiness is, you will never be unhappy.

Q: If you strip the body of all the psychological factors and attributes, would you say that there is no difference between a human being and an animal?

U.G.: Not at all. We are all like the animals. We are not different, nor we are created for any grander purpose than the mosquito that is sucking your blood.

Q: Is there any apparent difference between a human being and the normal sensate animal?

U.G.: It is thinking that has separated us from the other species on this planet. It is that thinking that we want to maintain. So it is that that is responsible for all the problems that the human mind (quote and unquote) has created.

Q: Of course, there is what is called purely biological survival. But hasn't thinking helped man to survive in a better way?

U.G.: As I said a while ago, it is thought which has separated us from the rest of the species. Through the help of thinking, it has become possible for us to create better conditions and survive longer than the other species.

Q: Why do you think that we live in this illusion, and why does it persist?

U.G.: The illusion persists because if the illusion comes to an end, what can be called clinical death will take place. So, if we give up one illusion, we will always replace it with another.

Q: Why?

U.G.: That is the thing that gives us the feeling of conquering the inevitable end called death. That is the only death that is there. Otherwise there is no such ting as death at all. And death is the end of the illusion, end of the fear, end of the knowledge that we have of ourselves and of the world around us.

Q: Now this raises the question as to what intelligence is. There is this natural intelligence of the body, which we talked about, with the help of which the harmonious and interrelated functions of the body are carried out. But is there an area wherein intelligence has a function other than the physical?

U.G.: No, you see the body does not want to know anything. The body does not want to learn anything. The intelligence that is nesessary for its survival is already there. We have, fortunately or unfortunately as the case may be, acquired what is called the intellect. Through the constant use and reshaping of thought we have acquired this intellect. Through the help of that intellect it has become possible for us to live longer than the other species. This in its own way is the cause of the destruction of the whole structure that we have created for our survival. There is no way of escaping from this fact that the acquired intellect, which is the product of our thinking, has helped us to survive longer than the other species.

Q: You mean to say that the intelligence that we have is in no way distinct or distinguishable from the animal intelligence?

U.G.: Probably in us the functioning of the body and of the brain is more evolved than in the case of animals. It does not mean that we are any better than the other species. If what they say is true, the human body, when broken into its constituent elements, is no different from the tree out there or the mosquito that is sucking your blood. Basically, it is exactly the same. The proportion of the elements may be higher in one case and lesser in the case of the other. You have eighty percent of water in the body, and there is eighty percent of water in the trees and eighty percent on this planet. So that is the reason why I maintain that we are nothing but a fortuitous concourse of atoms. If and when death takes place, the body is reshuffled, and then these atoms are used to maintain the energy levels in the universe. Other than that there is no such thing as death to this body.

Q: Is the human brain more sensitive than, say, the tree?

U.G.: If what they say is true, then probably the dog is far more intelligent than most of the human beings in our midst today, including me.

Q: Maybe.

U.G.: The animals don't try to change anything. That is the most important thing that we have to understand. The demand to bring about a change in us is the cultural input. What is there to be changed? That is my basic question. Is there anything to be changed, radically or otherwise? I don't know. So we have to find out, for ourselves and by ourselves, "What is there? Is there an entity there? Is there a self there? Is there an 'I' there?" My answer is, "No". What is seen or felt there is created by the knowledge we have of that, the knowledge of the self, the knowledge of the 'I', the knowledge of the entity there that is passed on to us from generation to generation. All that is the cultural.

Q: Is there not a communication here between us – the two individuals?

U.G.: Do you think that there is any communication between us? Are we trying to establish any communication here?

Q: No, essentially not. It is more a relationship.

U.G.: No. As long as you and I use the instrument that we are using to communicate with each other, no understanding is possible. You are always translating every statement of mine within the framework of knowledge that you have – that is what I call your reference point.

Q: The fact that we are talking, don't you think, shows that there is a physical or physiological relationship?

U.G.: That relationship is already there. So what separates you from me and me from you is the knowledge we have. But now we are trying to establish a sort of relationship on a different level. But knowledge is not the instrument for doing it, and there is no other instrument. If that is not the instrument and there is no other instrument, no understanding is necessary. That is the understanding, which somehow dawned on me – that there is nothing to understand. How it occurred I really don't know, and I have no way of knowing it. I have no way of helping somebody to understand that that is not the instrument and there is no other instrument. No instrument is necessary for us to create the realization that there is nothing to understand.

Q: There are various gurus who say that there is a soul or self....

U.G.: I know that. That is why even a saint like Ramana Maharshi, when people pestered him with all kinds of questions like, "What would you suggest for us to do?" threw back the question, "Who am I?" Even this question is not an intelligent question, because we assume both that there is some 'I' there, the nature of which we do not know, and that we have to inquire into its nature. As far as I am concerned, the only 'I' that I know of is the first person singular pronoun. I did not succeed and I don't think I will ever succeed in finding out for myself that there is any other 'I' than the 'I', which is used for the simple purpose of communication to separate you from me. I say, "I", and "You".

Q: The consciousness of the body....

U.G.: The consciousness of the body does not exist. There is no such thing as consciousness at all. The one thing that helps us to become conscious of the nonexistent body for all practical purpose is the knowledge that is given to us. Without that knowledge you have no way of creating your body and experiencing it. I am questioning the very idea of consciousness, let alone the subconscious, the unconscious, the different levels of consciousness, and higher states of consciousness. I don't see that there is any such thing as consciousness. I become conscious of this [*touching the arm of chair*] only through the knowledge that I have of it. The touch does not tell me anything except when I translate it within the framework of knowledge. Otherwise, I have no way of experiencing that touch at all. The way these senses are operating here is quite different from the way we are made to believe. The eye is looking at the movement of your hand, and is not saying anything about that activity, except observing what is going on there.

Q: But you can feel....

U.G.: No. Feeling is also a translation. This touch does not say anything about the touch *per se* except through the help of the knowledge that we have. You have no way of experiencing the fact that this is 'soft' or 'hard' except through the knowledge that you have of it. I don't know if it makes any sense to you.

Q: It makes sense to me. But it seems to me that when you touch there is a sensation in the body also.

U.G.: No. That sensation is through the sense of touch. It is translated by the activity of memory, the neurons, or whatever you like to call them, and only then you say that it is soft and not hard. So, you can kid yourself by telling yourself that this touch is one with feeling and not just a simple touch. But all that is superimposed on that.

Q: Can you tell me a little bit more about touch?

U.G.: If it is left purely on the physiological level there is no reaction on your part.

Q: Which part of it?

U.G.: That is the physical response. It is not translated. Probably that is a kind of pleasure for the body. I don't know. I have no way of finding out, whether that is the response of pleasure or a purely physical response to the touch. When people ask me, "Why do you smile"? I say that it is just a response like any other response to a stimulus. "Why do you move your hand?" "Why do you make many gestures?" You may call all these mere gestures, but they may be there because you feel that you are not expressing yourself adequately. You are backing your statements with these gestures. That is only a mode of communication. We all started that way and slowly developed language. But still you feel that you are not able to communicate things, convey to your fellow beings, whatever you are trying to say. That is why you have these different gestures to back up and strengthen what you are trying to communicate to others. In India they have one kind of gestures, and Americans have a different kind of gestures. Probably even these gestures or movements of hands are transmitted through the genes.

You know I met a lady in Italy. She was separated from her husband immediately after she gave birth to her son. They never met for twenty years. The mother told us that she always observed that the boy's gestures were no different from the gestures of her husband. Of course, this may not prove anything but merely suggests that even these might have been transmitted through the genes. We don't know what part the genes play and how the whole thing is transmitted from generation to generation.

Q: All this boils down to one thing, that is, that everything in us is just physical.

U.G.: I have no way of knowing it. Even the idea of separating the body and talking about it in terms of pure and simple physical responses may be misleading. I really don't know.

Q: Are you a materialist?

U.G.: I don't know. People call me a materialist. People even go to the extent of calling me an atheist just because I say that God is irrelevant. But that does not mean that I am an atheist. So I am not interested in what kind of labels they stick on me. Believe it or not: it does not make one bit of difference to me. I am not trying to convince you or win you over to anything.

When once the demand to bring about a change and to be different from what actually is there is absent, what you are left with is something, which you can never experience. That is the reason why I said that I am just an ordinary man. But people for their own reasons want to fit me into a framework of this, that, and a hundred different things. I say that I am just an ordinary man. Everybody thinks that I am not an ordinary man.

Lost in the Jungle

The demand to be prepared for all future actions and all situations is the cause of our problems. Every situation is so different; and our attempt to be prepared for all those situations is the one that is responsible for our not being able to deal with situations as they arise.

Q : You say that the humankind is no more important than the garden slug. Will you please comment on that?

U.G.: It is useless to speculate about it, but for some reason we are made to believe, or we have accepted the belief that has been passed on to us from generation to generation, that we are here for some grander purpose, for a nobler purpose than the other species on this planet. I maintain that we are here for no grander purpose than that of the garden slug out there or the mosquito that is sucking your blood.

I don't know that whether there is any such thing as evolution. Those who talk about evolution have made us believe that there is such a thing. We are told that if we look at the animal species that we have in this planet, there is only one and a half percent of what existed before. It you take the plants into consideration, what we have on this planet is only half a percent of what existed before. What, therefore, makes you think that the human species is more important than the other species that have become extinct? What has made it possible for us to survive, go on, and maintain the human species on this planet longer than others, is thought. It is thought that has made it possible for us to live longer than the other species.

Q : Thought has made it possible?

U.G.: But that is our enemy. Thought is our enemy. In the long run, our belief, hope, or faith that thought will help us by freeing us from the problems that it has created is just wishful thinking.

Q : How has it helped us to live longer than the other species? How can it be an impediment?

U.G.: Thought is a protective mechanism. It is interested in protecting something. We use thought for the purpose of maintaining the continuity of thought. Anything that has come out of thought is protective in its nature. It is not interested in protecting the life around us. It has isolated us from the rest of the species on this planet. It has given us the idea that we are something different, that the whole thing is created for our purpose, and that we have a right to take advantage of this superiority over others, to do whatever we want to do on this planet.

Q : Would it be possible to have thought without these ideas and still take advantage of nature?

U.G.: I maintain and very often say that thought in its birth, in its content, in its expression, and in its action is fascist. It is very aggressive. I use the word "fascist" not really in the sense that the politicians use, but to mean that thought is very aggressive. Our very demand to understand nature's laws is to use them for the purpose of maintaining the continuity of thought. All the talk that thought is altruistic and that we are curious to know the laws of nature just for the sake of knowing them is bluff. The very motivation, the drive behind our demand to understand the laws of nature is to use them for the purpose of continuing the human species at the expense of every other form of life on this planet.

Q : What would this human species have been if we did not have this kind of thought?

U.G.: Probably we would have become extinct and nature would have created a better form of human species on this planet. We would do anything that the animals would not do. The survival of one form of life at the expense of another form of life is a fact in nature. But we kill other species for an idea.

Q : We also kill ourselves for an idea.

U.G.: Certainly, and we kill others too. But that kind of thing you don't see happening in other forms of life, other species on this planet. We kill for an idea. The whole foundation of our culture and civilization is built on the idea of killing and being killed, first in the name of God as symbolized by all the religious institutions, and in the name of political ideologies as symbolized by the state. The whole foundation of culture is built on the idea of killing and being killed.

Q : We don't really admit that. We say that our cultures are based on our ideas of harmony.

U.G.: I do not think so. We are moving progressively in the direction of destroying everything. We somehow have tremendous faith that the thought, which has helped us to create everything that you see and are very proud of, will help us to change the course of events. This faith, I maintain, is misplaced. Somehow we have a faith that this instrument, thought, which has helped us to be what we are today, will somehow help us to create a better, happier life on this planet.

Q : But how do we get out of this if it is heading down a path of destruction?

U.G.: Everything you discover is adding to the momentum of destruction. Everything because, the drive behind that discovery is to use it for purposes of maintaining the continuity, the status quo.

Q : Is there any possibility that the human species will figure that out in time and change course, and if it does change course, what kind of change would it be?

U.G.: I say the chances are slim to none. We are doomed, you see. [*Laughs*] As I said at the beginning, we are lost in the jungle; we have tried every possible means of escape. But still, somehow, there is a faint hope that maybe there is some way we can get out of this jungle. But we just have to stand still and let things happen.

Q : But how can we stand still? What is it that will help us to stand still?

U.G.: You cannot stand still. You cannot stand still because of the fear that we will be lost and lost forever. But we don't seem to have the feeling that there is not a damn thing that we can do to get out of this jungle.

Q : Do *you* stand still in this way?

U.G.: Yes, certainly. Then what is there takes over and probably enables you to live in the midst of all these brutalities. That life has a charm of its own. It will not bring you in conflict with society at all. You don't even want to change anything. The demand to change is born out of your isolation. When once you think that you can bring about a change in yourself, the demand to change the world is also there. But this human body is not interested in learning or knowing anything. All that is necessary for the survival of this living organism is already there. There is a tremendous intelligence there, and all that we have gathered and acquired through our intellect is no match for that.

Q : ...to the intelligence of the body?

U.G.: Yes, the intelligence of the body. It knows. One of the things that I always emphasize and try to put across to those who are interested is that the human brain is not interested in anything that we are interested in, what the culture has imposed on us, in any of its ideation and mentations. The brain is so dull; you will be surprised. It is not interested in any experience of any kind. What it is interested in is to help the body function intelligently and sanely.

Q : You mean the brain?

U.G.: Yes, the brain. But unfortunately, we have put that brain to a use for which nature has not intended it. The brain is not a creator. It is only a reactor; it reacts to stimuli. The mechanism that we have implanted in it as it were, through our education and culture, has made us believe that it is a creator. All the thoughts that we are thinking are not self-generated. They are not spontaneous. They always come from outside, and the brain is there only to translate this sensation – the translation that is necessary for the survival of this living organism. It is not interested in any of the spiritual experiences or anything that the mind is interested in (mind, quote and unquote). In fact, I don't see any mind there at all. The mind is interested only in sensuality. It is born out of sensuality. It maintains its continuity in the field of sensuality. So all religious experiences of any kind are sensual in their nature. It is only the mind that is interested in spiritual experiences – bliss, compassion, truth, reality, and all those kinds of things. But the body, the living organism, is not interested in any of those things but only to respond to stimuli.

Q : If the brain is created with the intelligence of the body, what is the creativity that is associated with thought?

U.G.: The creativity that you are talking about is totally unrelated to the creativity of life.

Q : What is the source of creativity, and is there any creativity in nature?

U.G.: There is no creativity in the sense in which w are using the word 'creativity' – language, the creativity of thought, the creativity of this, that, or the other. Life is creative in the sense that it does not use any model. Anything we call creative is an imitation, copy of something that is already there. It is second hand. You cannot say that something which nature has created is not up to the point. I don't even see any blue print there. Whatever blue print is there is already there in the cell. Everything that is there now was there in that single cell. Everything is genetically controlled.

Q : There is nothing you can change – a little shade here and there?

U.G.: The idea that there is something that we can do to bring about a change within us and change in the world has placed us in a situation where we are left with a hope that somehow this may happen. You live in that hope and die in that hope.

Q : Is change possible?

U.G.: What kind of change are you interested in? Change is possible in the physical world. For example, if you are not interested in the shape of a stubbed nose, you can go to a plastic surgeon and change it into an aquiline nose. If you feel that it is fashionable to have that then there is a possibility of availing the help of a plastic surgeon. Or, through genetic engineering it will be possible for us to bring about a change in behaviour patterns. I do not claim to have a special insight into the nature of things or an understanding of the workings of nature more than anybody else, but this is what I have discovered for myself. I don't care whether you accept what I am saying or not. It stands or falls by itself. I don't care for even the biologists, the psychologists, or scientists in general. If they brush this aside and say this is all absolute rubbish, it is fine with me. One of these days they are going to discover these things anyway.

Q : Well, how does one discover that?

U.G.: You see, the discovery is not within the framework of thinking. In other words, there is no such thing as discovery. Discovery is a wrong word.

Q : Wrong word?

U.G.: You experience what you already know. Otherwise, there is no experience at all. There is no such thing as a new experience.

The so-called epoch-making discoveries in the field of science are not really epoch-making discoveries. Take, for example, Newtonian physics. It works very well for some countries. But that very Newtonian physics proved to be a stumbling block for making a quantum jump, if I may use the word, quote and unquote. Somehow, somebody like Einstein was lucky to take the lead and discover something different.

Q : Did he really discover something different?

U.G.: Actually, it is not different. Unless you link up these two things – what was there before, and what you think you have discovered – there is no point in talking about that at all. The scientist is interested in linking up these things and producing some results. Otherwise the discovery has no value at all. Newtonian physics is valid, functional, and true within its own framework. But this same Newtonian physics is not so true, not so valid, compared to what we have (or rather, Einstein has) since discovered, namely, the 'theory of Relativity'. Of course, Newtonian physics is still valid within the framework of the scientific thinking of man. After all, we admire all these people and regard them with prestigious honour – the Nobel Prize, this, that, and the other. Do you know the reason why? It is because of the technology that has become possible through discoveries of these people. Otherwise, there is no such thing as true discovery. There is no such thing as pure science at all. I may be making a lot of dogmatic statements, but my statements stand or fall by themselves.

Q : But there must be ...

U.G.: Why do you say there must be? There may not be. Then where do we go from 'There may not be'?

Q : You have apparently had some experiences that helped you see things more clearly. How does that help? Can you talk about your experience?

U.G.: I very often use the phrase 'stumbled into'. Somehow, somewhere along my journey of discovery, it occurred to me that this instrument which we have been using, what we call the intellect, is not really the instrument to understand anything. But I was very clear that the only instrument we have to understand anything is the intellect, and that there is no other instrument. So, the whole of our discovery is nothing but improving...

Q : Improving the intellect...

U.G.: Sharpening that intellect. That is all that is there. So, this (the intellect) has not helped me to understand the living problems of my life, nor understand myself and the world around me. The understanding that this is not the instrument and that there is no other instrument somehow dawned on me.

Q : ...that the human being does not possess an instrument to understand.

U.G.: There is no instrument to understand anything other than this instrument. That knocks off the whole foundation of intuition or any other way of understanding the reality surrounding us. There is nothing to understand. That is why I maintain that there is no such thing as reality at all, let alone the ultimate reality. You have no way of experiencing the reality of anything – the reality that we have so much taken for granted. We don't experience anything other than what we know.

Q : So we are just experiencing the past. It is repetitive.

U.G.: It is a repetitive process experiencing the same thing over and over again. That is why we are born hoping that one day we will find something extraordinary, some new experience. The moment you say that it is something, which you have not experienced before, that it is a new experience, it means that it has already become part of the past experiencing mechanism.

Q : Are you bored?

U.G.: Boredom is there only when you think that there is something more interesting, more purposeful, more meaningful that you could do than what you are doing.

Q : Well, you don't feel that you can...

U.G.: That is all there is for me.

Q : How did you get out of this boredom?

U.G.: I wish I knew. That is why I used the phrase 'stumbled into'. There is no way I can communicate this to anybody. Anybody who comes and listens to me and tries to understand what I am trying to put across is wasting his time, because there is no way you can listen to anything without interpretation. The interpreter is the reference point, which is you. You are the product of the totality of all the thoughts, experiences, and feelings of every form of life that existed before you. Thought is only interested in maintaining its continuity and status quo. It does not want any change. It says that it wants to change but the change that it is interested in is only to maintain its continuity, its status quo. Although things are changing constantly, it does not want to accept anything that will disturb its status quo. Also the reference point is strengthened and fortified by interpreting what I am saying to you.

Q : But it is completely stuck.

U.G.: You don't want to accept that any attempt on your part to get out of that trap in which you find yourself is strengthening the shackles. And there is no way out.

Q : So we have to accept that we are stuck?

U.G.: Accepting means that you are sick and tired of doing anything. But saying that does not really mean anything.

Q : So we have to have a purpose in life?

U.G.: Why do we look for a purpose or meaning? Why?

Q : Why do we, you see? That is the question. Why do we?

U.G.: You tell me, why do we? Why should there be any meaning? The question. "How to live?" is totally unrelated to the functioning of this living organism. It is living all the time. It doesn't have to ask the question, "How to live?" "How to live?" is superimposed on the living organism.

Q : And the search for meaning is absurd...?

U.G.: Obviously you do not see any meaning. You do not see any purpose in life. Obviously you don't see. [*Laughs*] I don't mean only you. I mean people. To me to ask that question is so silly, so meaningless, and so absurd – "What is the meaning of life?" It is not life that we are really interested in but living. The problem of living has become a very tiring business – to live with somebody else, to live with our feelings, to live with our ideas. In other words, it is the value system that we have been thrown into. You see, the value system is false.

Q : ... like glue all over.

U.G.: We are trying to fit ourselves into that value system which is totally false. It is falsifying you. But you are not ready to accept that it is falsifying you. You throw a lot of energy into this business of fitting yourself into that framework or value system.

Q : How does one get to that point wherein they are willing to accept that this is false?

U.G.: 'How' implies that you want to know from somebody.

Q : You mean asking the question...

U.G.: That is adding momentum to that – to know, to know, and to know. That is why we always ask that question, 'how?'. 'How?' means you want to know. What is this 'you', as you experience yourself? The 'you' as you know yourself is a product of the momentum of that knowledge that is passed on to us. It has this question that you think is a very intelligent question. Through your demand for an answer to that question it wants to know how to add momentum to that knowledge.

Q : So, it is a trick. It is falsifying us.

U.G.: It knows that by asking the question it can add momentum to itself. It is not 'you', because 'you' don't exist. There is no individual there at all. Culture, society, or whatever you want to call it, has created 'you' and 'me' for the sole purpose of maintaining its own continuity. But at the same time we are made to believe that you have to become an individual. These two things have created this neurotic situation for us. There is no such thing as an individual, and there is no such thing as freedom of action. I am not talking of a fatalistic philosophy or any such thing. It is this fact that is frustrating us. The demand to fit ourselves into that value system is using a tremendous amount of energy, and there is nothing we can do to deal with the living problems here. All the energy is being consumed by the demands of the culture or society, or whatever you want to call it, to fit you into the framework of that value system. In the process, we are not left with any energy to deal with the other problems. But these problems, that is, the living problems, are very simple.

Q : In what way?

U.G.: To survive in this world is not a difficult problem, you see. But what is demanding is the value system. Our efforts to fit ourselves into that value system are consuming a tremendous amount of energy.

Q : But what happens if you just don't fit yourself into the value system?

U.G.: I am not in conflict with this society. You seem to be in conflict with this society, but I am not, because it cannot be any different, since I have found out that there is no way I can bring about a change in it. You want to bring about a change in the world. You see, the problem is a problem of relationship. It is just not possible to establish any relationship with anything around you, including your near and dear once, except on the level of what you can get out of the relationship. You see, the whole thing springs from this separation or isolation that human beings live in today. We are isolated from the rest of creation, the rest of life around us. We all live in individual frames. We try to establish a relationship at the level of "What do I get out of that relationship?" We use others to try and fill this void that is created as a result of our isolation.

We always want to fill this emptiness, this void, with all kinds of relationships with people around us. That is really the problem. We have to use everything, an idea, a person, anything we can get hold of, to establish relationships with others. Without relationships we are lost, and we don't see any meaning; we don't see any purpose. This is because your only interest is to create a purposeful and meaningful relationship with the individuals and the world around you. Therefore, you want to understand the reality of the world.

But there is nothing to understand. There is no such thing as reality at all. I have to accept the reality of the world as it is imposed on me by the society. Say, I call you a 'woman', I call this a 'bench', and I call this a 'tray'. Otherwise, we will not be able to function in this world sanely and intelligently. This kind of knowledge can be used only for the purposes of functioning in this world sanely and intelligently. Anything you do to understand the reality of the world is not going to be useful, helpful, or meaningful.

Death is a Reshuffling of Atoms

The belief in reincarnation is born out of the demand that something will continue after your so-called death. It is the same mechanism, which wants to know what will happen after death. For some reason that mechanism, that movement of thought, does not want to come to an end. But, if you want to know if there is anything beyond, you have to die now.

Q : How are you and I different? In perceptions? Or is there any other difference?

U.G.: The thought that I am different from you never, never enters my head. It is thinking that separates you and tells you that I am different from you; that I am functioning differently from you. But you and I are functioning in exactly the same way.

Q : ... except that I am thinking with thoughts in order to know.

U.G.: Yes, you want to know. The living organism is like a computer with an extraordinary intelligence; similar to the way that tape recorder is functioning. The recorder never asks the question, "How am I functioning?" All it needs is the energy there. The electricity is necessary for it's functioning. But here the energy is a sort of expression of life. Energy is already there. But you are all the time asking questions.

The thought that I am different from you never enters my head at all. If you ask me the question, "Are you not different from me?" all the knowledge that I have, that separates you and me, is already there in the computer. It tells me that you are a woman and I am a man, and you are more intelligent than I am. The whole series of ideas that are put into the computer comes into operation. Your question brings out the knowledge that is there, stored in the computer here [*pointing to himself*]. These are two computers talking, but you want to introduce an element, which is not part of the functioning of this living organism. That is why you begin to think that there must be something different here [in U.G.].

Q : So, I am making the separation?

U.G.: You are making the separation. It is the very question that separates us. But actually there are no questions at all. All the questions are born out of the answers we already have. They are not really the questions.

Q : So, actually, we should probably be keeping silent?

U.G.: You think that silence is a means to understand anything? It is the game of all these religious people. Through silence they feel they are communicating something. But in that silence no communication is necessary.

Q : What is the nature of intelligence? What does that word mean to you?

U.G.: The only meaning that I can come up with is what we find in the dictionary.

Q : Oh, well, there is a lot of intelligence in you ...

U.G.: I agree that you are more intelligent than I am. That is just because of our background and our hereditary differences.

Q : Is there any higher intelligence?

U.G.: You are more intelligent than I am. You see this is something that can be measured. We have certain yardsticks in the world that say that you are more intelligent than I am. Those are acceptable to me. But any attempt on my part to improve my intelligence, change it, modify it, make it better, would consume tremendous amount of energy. That is all. You see, without that, what you are left with is something extraordinary. It is not interested in comparing itself with your intellect or anything. It is not a question of accepting that I am a low-grade moron. "Acceptance" is not the word. When once it is a fact that there is no movement in any direction of improving, changing, evolving into anything different or better; then what is there is something extraordinary. It is unique in its own way. Every individual is unique. Nature creates perfect species and not perfect individuals.

Q : Nature?

U.G.: Perfect species, not perfect individuals. Perfect individuals are created by the religious thinking of man. We have put before ourselves the models of Jesus and Buddha and all these religious teachers. It would be a horrible world if this planet were to be only full of teachers.

Q : It would be horrible and terrible.

U.G.: …like filling this whole earth with only roses of one kind. It would be a horrible place. That is what education is doing to us.

Q : So, the individual isn't perfect but the species is …?

U.G.: Every human being is different. That is all I am saying. There is nobody like you anywhere in this world. I tell you, nobody! I am talking physiologically, you know. But we ignore that, and try to put everybody in a common mould and create what we call the greatest common factor. All the time you are trying to educate them and fit them into the value system. If that value system does not work, naturally revolutions take place. The whole idea of restructuring is nothing but a revaluation of the old value system. Revolution only means revaluation of our value system. It is the same thing. After a while things settle down, and then they go at it again. There is no improvement again. Or there is a slight improvement. But it is a modified continuity of the same. In that process what horrors we have committed, you know! Is it really worth all that? But you seem to think that it is. After killing so many people you go back to the same system, the same technique. What is the point? But we will keep going that way.

Q : Can I ask you about death? What is death?

U.G.: In nature there is no such thing as death but only a reshuffling of atoms. [*Laughs*]

Q : What happens?

U.G.: The balance of energy in nature has to be maintained for some reason. I don't know why. So death occurs only when there is a need for the atoms to maintain the balance of energy in the universe. It is nothing but a reshuffling of atoms. This organism has no way of finding out that it was born at a particular point of time and is going to die at another point of time, and also that it is living at this moment and not dead. The knowledge we have of this living organism – the birth, the death, and all that – is absent here [*pointing to himself*].

Q : So you are saying you cannot know whether you are alive or dead?

U.G.: No way, if you ask me the question, "Are you alive?" I would say that I am alive. Because the question is born out of the idea of how a living human being functions, acts, and thinks. That is an idea. So, naturally, if you ask me a question, "Are you alive or dead?" I would say I am very much alive, because that question brings all the knowledge that we have about the behaviour patterns of living human beings. But we have no way of experiencing the fact that this is a living thing. You see, thought is dead. It is trying to capture something that is living, pulsating.

Q : So thought is trying to experience something it has no capacity to experience?

U.G.: No capacity, because it may be burnt in that process. If you touch a live wire, you are finished. So thought doesn't want to touch it; it wants to play with it, and put on gloves and talk about it.

Q : Does the body have the understanding minus the thoughts?

U.G.: The heart does not for a moment know that it is pumping blood. It is not asking the question, "Am I doing it right?" it is just functioning. It does not ask the question, "Is there any purpose?"

To me, that question has no meaning. The questions, "Is there any meaning?" "Is there any purpose?" take away the living quality of life. You are living in a world of ideas.

Q : Is there life after death?

U.G.: Anything I say would not be of much interest to people. When people ask me whether there is any such thing as reincarnation, my answer is that there is reincarnation for those who believe in it, and there is no reincarnation for those who do not believe in it. It is not a clever answer because it is the belief, which is important. If you ask a fundamental question, "Is there any such thing as reincarnation as the other laws in nature like gravity?" my answer would be negative, a definite, "No". It is not as much part of nature as gravity is. But if you want to believe it is so, it is a different matter. The belief in reincarnation is born out of the demand that something will continue after your so-called death. It is the same mechanism, which wants to know what will happen after death. For exactly the same reason you are asking the question, "Is there any meaning, is there any purpose in life?" For some reason that mechanism, that movement of thought, does not want to come to an end. You have people dying there. So, the belief that there is a centre here, that there is a spirit here, that there is a soul here, is what is responsible for that belief that there must be something beyond. But, if you want to know if there is anything beyond, you have to die now. When the question or belief about that comes to an end, death will take place here right now. Clinical death will take place. Then the questions whether there is an afterlife would not at all arise because the living organism has no way of knowing that it is alive.

Q : And you said that those who believe in reincarnation ...

U.G.: The belief has to go. The end of belief is death.

Q : So death ends all beliefs...?

U.G.: But you replace one belief with another, one illusion with another illusion. That is all that we are doing.

Q : I wanted to ask you another question...

U.G.: The answer will be the same. [*Laughs*]

Sex is Painful to the Body

Sexuality, if it is left to itself, as it is in the case of other species, other forms of life, is merely a biological need, because the living organism has this object to survive and produce one like itself. Anything you superimpose on that is totally unrelated to the living organism. But we have turned that, what you call sexual activity, which is biological in its nature, into a pleasure movement.

Q : I wanted to ask you about love.

U.G.: Oh, my God! Oh, my God! [*Laughs*]

Q : I know what people say about love.

U.G.: What do *you* think about it?

Q : I don't know.

U.G.: I don't know either.

Q : Is there another...?

U.G.: There must be two, you know. I love somebody and somebody else loves me. Wherever there is division, there can't be love. We are trying to bridge this gap, which is horrible for us, which has no meaning, which is demanding something from us, with this fancy idea that there must be love between these two individuals.

Q : Between whatever...?

U.G.: Between whatever – I love my country, I love my dog, I love my wife, and what else. What is the difference – whether I love my wife, I love my country, or I love my dog? [*Both laugh*] This may sound very cynical to you. The fact of the matter is that there is no difference. You love *your* country, I love *my* country, and there is war.

Q : So, there is no love? Love is another of these thoughts?

U.G.: Yes, created by thought.

Q : Can the body not love?

U.G.: It does not love itself. There is no separateness here.

Q : Is that all there is to love?

U.G.: You want me to give a positive answer to your question. I am not trying to evade. This is not a political interview. I am not dodging. I don't want to give any clever or diplomatic answer. Why are we asking about love?

Q : Well, human beings ask about that...

U.G.: Obviously, our relationships are not so loving. So, we want to, somehow, make them into loving affairs, loving relationships.

Q : So it makes us feel that...

U.G.: What an amount of energy we are putting into making our relationship into a loving thing! It is a battle; it is a war. It is like preparing yourself all the time for war hoping that there will be peace, eternal peace, or this or that. You are tired of this battle, and you even settle for that horrible, non-loving relationship. And you hope and dream one day it will be nothing but love. "Love thy neighbour as thyself - " in the name of that how many millions of people have been killed? More than all the recent wars put together. How can you love thy neighbour as thyself? It is just not possible.

Q : Do you think it is impossible for any human being?

U.G.: Obviously; otherwise, why are so many people, women, children, and helpless people killed?

Q : No. But there are also good neighbours you know.

U.G.: Yes, yes, you know. [*Both laugh*] When once love fails to establish the perfect ideal relationship between two individuals what we are left with is hate. If not hate, it is antipathy, apathy, or what other words...? My vocabulary is very poor.

Q : That is good enough... What about sexuality? Is that just a reproductive function or does it help some other meaningful...?

U.G.: Sexuality, if it is left to itself, as it is in the case of other species, other forms of life, is merely a biological need, because the living organism has this object to survive and produce one like itself. Anything you superimpose on that is totally unrelated to the living organism. But we have turned that, what you call sexual activity, which is biological in its nature, into a pleasure movement. I am not saying anything against the pleasure movement. It has become possible for us to have sex at any time we want through the help of thought.

Q : So, that is one of the ways thought has separated us from the rest of the world?

U.G.: Then it is a bore again. We have to write books – the *Joy of Loving*, the *Kama Sutra*, and all kinds of books – and make it interesting. It is not possible for animals to have sex at any time they want. Animals use it only for reproduction. Not that they 'use' it, but it is for the purposes of reproducing their own species. It is not a pleasure movement in their case. I am not saying anything against the pleasure movement. I am not interested in saying that you should condemn that or become promiscuous or use sex as a means of spiritual attainment. No.

Q : So, you say sex cannot be a spiritual experience?

U.G.: It is a very simple functioning of the living organism. The religious man has turned that into something big, and concentrated on the control of sex. After that the psychologists have turned that into something extraordinary. All commercialism is related to sex. How do you think it will fall into its proper place?

Q : It is used to sell...

U.G.: Yes, sure. I am not against that. Please don't get me wrong. I am just pointing out the use to which we are putting that simple biological function. I am not condemning it. It is there, you see. Your talk of that as an expression of love has no meaning to me.

Q : Then there is no relation between love and sex?

U.G.: No.

Q : That is really devastating! Most of the world for sure thinks that love without sex is like a cold shake-hand.

U.G.: We would love to put it that way because it is very comforting. If sex is used only for the biological purpose, as I said, it is not really a devastating situation. If you leave it as it is, it wouldn't be so horrible, the way you would like to put it. It would fall into its proper place. That is why we have invented all these other things – God, truth, and reality – which are nothing but ultimate pleasures.

Q : Is that a goal too?

U.G.: Whether you are here, in Russia, or anywhere else, the one thing that anybody and everybody wants in this world is to have happiness without one moment of unhappiness, pleasure without pain. That is just not possible, because this living organism does not know what pleasure is, what happiness is.

Q : The organism does not know what pleasure is?

U.G.: It doesn't even want it.

Q : It wants but it hasn't ...

U.G.: It doesn't want it, because all these pleasurable sensations disturb it. The moment there is a pleasurable sensation, the demand to extend it longer and longer is there. That is why there is this tremendous frustration there. You want to make it possible for everybody that he should always be happy and that he should have only pleasant or pleasurable sensations and not any painful ones. It may be possible through some drugs like "ecstasy", but for how long?

Q : What happens if you indulge in such things?

U.G.: In the long run it destroys the sensitivity of the body.

Q : How do you say that?

U.G.: You are not in living touch with anything there.

Q : ...so thought is separating us from the natural way?

U.G.: Yes, the natural way.

A Freak of Nature

Even the idea that you should control your thought in order to be in a thoughtless or peaceful state is created by thought, so that it can maintain its continuity through some petty little experience, through some thoughtless state you are interested in.

Q : I want to ask you about your personal experiences, and I know you don't want to talk about them...

U.G.: Very often people ask me such questions. But let me tell you, whatever has happened to me has happened despite everything I did. Some of the biographers who are keen on writing the story of my life are very anxious to know what I did, what I did not do, what helped me to stumble into this kind of thing, assuming for a moment that some event, occurrence, or happening in my life put me where I am today. But this is not something valid and true. You have to accept my word. If you don't accept what I say, it doesn't matter. Whatever had happened before whatever happened to me, all the events in my life before that have no relevance to the way I am functioning now. And from that moment on, there is no story to tell. I am here today talking to you; tomorrow I will be somewhere else talking to my friends; and the day after tomorrow I will be in England. That is all. So, there is nothing that anybody can tell about me after that.

I am a public man. I am here any moment you want to see what I am doing, all 24 hours. I have no private life of my own. Any time you want to know what U. G. is doing, at that particular time, in that particular situation, you can see. So, there is no story to tell. That is the reason why I maintain that whatever has happened to me happened despite everything I did. But you are interested in finding out how and why that particular thing I am talking about has happened to me and not to everybody. You want to establish a cause and effect relationship and make it possible for everybody to stumble into this kind of thing. That is something, which cannot be produced or reproduced on an assembly line. It is a freak of nature.

Q : But we would be interested in knowing what the freak of nature was in U.G..

U.G.: Even wanting to understand that has no meaning to you. You just leave it there. There are so many freakish things there in nature. If you try to copy them, you are lost. You are in the same situation as before. Even nature has no use for this body [*pointing to his body*]. It has discarded it because it cannot reproduce something like this either physically or otherwise.

Q : So you have been discarded by nature?

U.G.: Yes, discarded by nature. How can you turn this into a model? That is what we have done to all those discarded people whom we should have discarded for good.

Q : How many?

U.G.: I don't know. Probably you can count on your fingers.

Q : The people who have had ...

U.G.: I don't know. I can't say. I am not interested in saying anything about them.

Q : But what about all the ideas – the religious ideas throughout the ages, spiritual ideas? Is there any tradition that you know besides...?

U.G.: I can say one thing, that is, all that is false as far as I am concerned and it has falsified me. So, don't ask me the question, "How can all of them be false?" No, that is not the point. I don't want to be falsified because that is not the way I function. I wanted to relate whatever was their state of being with the way I was functioning, and then struggled and struggled so hard.

Q : You struggled...?

U.G.: It got me nowhere. So, there is no way you can reject it, because it is that which has created what you call 'you'.

Q : What created me?

U.G.: The value system has created 'you', and there is no way you can free yourself from that. Anything you do to free yourself from that value system is adding momentum to it. This is the one thing that never occurred to me at that time. What I was saying a while ago was that thought couldn't be used as an instrument. You can use it to control, shape, and mould the value system. But you have no way of freeing yourself from it through thought. Even the idea that you should control your thought in order to be in a thoughtless or peaceful state is created by thought, so that it can maintain its continuity through some petty little experience, through some thoughtless state you are interested in.

Q : What about these states of higher consciousness that people speak of?

U.G.: If there is any such thing, you are an expression of that. Why should nature or something, some cosmic power, if there is one in this world, need the help of somebody to express itself and help others? I don't see any need. If there is anything like that, you are as much an expression of it as any of these claimants. Every dog, every cat, every pig, every cow that you see, the garden slug there, you, me, and everybody, even Chenghiz Khan and Hitler, are an expression of that same thing. They might have acted in a different way. You and I may act in a different way. But we are all expressions of the same thing, and there is no need for that to use any channel other than you. You are an expression of that.

But I even question consciousness itself. There is no such thing as consciousness at all, let alone higher consciousness, super consciousness or cosmic consciousness. All these notions are created by thought. We were discussing this morning the idea that consciousness is a concept. You become conscious of things only through the help of knowledge. I become conscious of you only through the knowledge I have about you, which has been passed on to me. The fact that I say that you are a woman, that you are an intelligent woman, and that you are a pretty woman – all this is part of that knowledge. Otherwise I am not separate from you. There is no way I can look at you and say anything about you. The eyes act only as cameras.

Q : So there is no way you can perceive anything except through the knowledge…?

U.G.: Knowledge creates images. But there is no way that this physical functioning can create any image. The moment I turn to this side, the whole thing on the other side is wiped out.

Q : I disappear. [*Laughs*]

U.G. : You disappear, because the eyes are not looking at you but at him or at that chair or at whatever they are focussing themselves on. But if he asks me, "Wasn't she pretty?" "pretty" is a word, not an image. Do you understand? "She is very 'sharp'". Another word. I will talk about you in words, and it is a word-picture. But the images, the physical images are totally absent. The so-called psychological images have no place in the scheme of things. The eyes are like a camera. If you turn the camera from what it is looking at to something else, the whole thing where it was focussed on earlier is wiped out. And what is there in the computer [*pointing to his head*] is only the word picture, and probably the sounds.

These days they are dictating to computers. They have problems of dealing with accent. Computers will have some difficulty there, for instance, when an Indian is speaking with an Indian accent. They will have to learn the accent. These days you don't have to type it. That is the way the sounds are registered here in this computer [*pointing to himself*]. The word-picture is here. That is all I give – a word-picture. If I am not looking at you, I cannot create any image, because the eye is not focussed on you. The problem is very simple. I don't know what you look like, as I have no way of creating the image inside of me. So, it ceases to be a problem. "I saw or meet an extraordinarily intelligent woman, a pretty woman - " what does that mean?

My daughter sometimes asks me. "See, I am your daughter, what does that mean to you?" It doesn't mean anything to me. If

I happen to be next to her and if somebody asks me, "Who is she?" I will say, "This is my daughter"; that is, whatever the dictionary meaning of the word is.

Q : ... that is there in our system.

U.G.: The image we have is superimposed on that word. That is really the problem. So, the physical images have to go fast. There is nothing that you can do about it. Nothing. Not a thing.

Q : What is physical? What is matter?

U.G.: You don't even know.

Q : No, I am asking you. How would you describe that?

U.G.: The same word that I use. You see, "This is my hand".

Q : Then what is matter? What is basic matter?

U.G.: There is no matter at all. Matter is thought. You see, if you touch something hard, the sense of touch does not say this is hard [*U.G. touches, the arm of the chair*]. But once you have the knowledge, the past knowledge, you say it is hard, because thought creates a space here and the enormous knowledge that I have about it....

Q : What is matter?

U.G.: What is matter? You want a definition? Thought creates matter.

Q : That is what I was wondering about.

U.G.: That is what I am saying.

Q : So, if we obliterate thought, matter would go too?

U.G.: Definitions are of no interest to me, because what is there is energy.

Q : We were talking about matter. Matter is created by thought. If we did not think…?

U.G.: Thought is matter.

Q : What about the dogs, which don't have thought?

U.G.: Probably they have some kind of thought. I don't know. But ours has become very complex and complicated.

Q : Is there thought, human thought, as part of this matter?

U.G.: There is no thought. There are only thoughts. Is there a thought there in you?

Q : Sure, we talk about it.

U.G.: No, is there a thought? At the very beginning I said the brain is not a creator. Thoughts are not spontaneous. They come from outside. You translate that particular noise [*noise of thunder*] with the help of the memory, which is neurons. They tell you that the noise is thunder. You recognize that. That is all there is to it – the information. What is thought? We ask that question because of the assumption that there is a thought that you want to know about. But what there is is only *about* thoughts – all the definitions. "Thought is matter", is a statement, which by itself has no meaning at all.

Q : This statement, "Thought is matter", has no meaning?

U.G.: Has no meaning at all. I have explained why thought is matter because …

Q : That has upset some physicists?

U.G.: We don't care about the physicists. But they also say that there is no such thing as thought, there is no such thing as matter, there is no such thing as space, and there is no such thing as time. But what is this entire time-and-space continuum? Such a continuum is necessary for them; otherwise their whole research collapses.

Is there space? No. There is no space. There is no way you can experience space. It is thought that creates it. Anything you say about space has no meaning. There is no way you can experience space at all. You can say there is no thought, there is no space, there is no matter, and there is no time. First, you create thought, then thought creates space, and then time is necessary to cover the distance, to experience the space, to capture it, and do something with it. So, then time comes in. But there is no time. The only time that is there is arbitrary. It is 11 p.m. here and 11 a.m. the next morning somewhere else. We are 12 hours behind. If you travel to or from India, you miss one day or gain one day.

All ideas of time, even those of chronological time, are arbitrary. All measurements are arbitrary. We accept them as workable, that is all. As a little boy asked a man, "Why should two and two be four?" The man brought four apples, four mangoes, four oranges, and four rupees. Said the boy, "I am not interested in that. Is there number two without number one, and one without two?" "Don't ask me those questions", the main said. There ends our mathematics, arithmetic. I take for granted that two and two is four. If you ask me for four dollars, I count and give you four dollars, four rupees, or four roubles, depending upon which country I happen to be at that particular time. Even in the area of counting, there is always a reference point.

When somebody quotes the price of a particular thing, we always think in terms of the currency we are familiar with. Even for the valuation of a thing, there is a reference point – the reference point is the dollar or the rupee or the pound as the case may be. So is there matter? Is there space? This is not metaphysics that I am talking about, much less what the physicists are talking about, i.e., the impossibilities of experiencing space. Without thought there is no way what you call 'you' can be separated. What you call 'you' is thought. There is no 'you' there other than this demand to experience space or matter or time, as the case may be. Thought has also created the idea of the timeless. All achievements are in time.

Q : Where do all these thoughts come from?

U.G.: They are all over. There is a thought sphere in which we are all functioning. But one question (I don't ask myself that question because there is no point in posing that question to myself, nor am I interested in finding an answer for it) for which the answer is not very clear is: do these thoughts come from outside passed on from generation to generation, or are they also transmitted through the genes? I have every reason to believe that the totality of knowledge is not only transmitted through our education in all forms, shape, sizes, and degrees, but also, to a greater extent, through the genes. Now they are saying that the capacity to learn not only languages but *a* language is genetically controlled.

Q : What do you think of the work that scientists are doing in genetic engineering?

U.G.: I am all for it, but if it is handed over to the state, they will use it to make people do things without any resistance. Now you have to educate them, teach them patriotism, make them salute the flag, go to the war field, and use guns. It takes decades to brainwash people either to believe in God or not to believe in God, to believe in democracy, to believe in Communism. But with genetics you don't have to do a thing. Just give a drug and they will go and kill. Even there, the first killing is all that is a problem; from then on, the killing is simpler. You ask any murderer. The first time you have the problem of killing, but from then on you act like a machine gun and kill people. It is a thoughtless action.

The basic question, which we all have to ask and should be interested in, is what kind of human being do we want on this planet? What kind? What do you want a human being to be? What is your answer? What you want can be created through the help of genes rather than through the process of educating people. You see, it takes years and years to make a man believe in something and free him from something else. If there is a tendency towards alcoholism, if there is a tendency to smoke, if there is a tendency to thieve, it is a lot easier to change that, for whatever reason, through the manipulation of the genes of that individual rather than giving him lectures on morality and teaching him. It takes years and years that way.

Q : So change can happen through biological manipulation.

U.G.: But when the knowledge acquired by genetics, or whatever you may call it, is passed on to the state, we are in trouble. After all, state patronage is necessary for them to carry on their research.

Q : Is it likely that it is going to become a function of the state?

U.G.: It will. You see, they will hand it over.

Q : At least in some places...

U.G.: Yes, everywhere; why "some places"? If you don't do it, some other country will do it.

Q : What you are saying is that there is a possibility of evolving a new species through the engineering of genes.

U.G.: Is there any such thing as evolution? I question even that. Darwin has put us all on the wrong track. He said that acquired characteristics are not transmitted from generation to generation. But that is no longer true now. For a hundred years we believed him. For a hundred years we also believed in the theories of Freud, who was a stupendous fraud.

Q : But for thousands of years there has been an acceptance of the belief in evolution.

U.G.: Now things are changing so fast that we are not able to keep pace with them. We have tremendous systems of communication now. Whatever is happening here is happening everywhere. They are able to see what is happening here and what is happening there in Bangladesh. Now the time factor has been reduced to a minimum through the help of modern communication techniques.

Q : But that is not evolution; that is just...

U.G.: No, it is not evolution. It is a trial-and-error process. You are perfecting the same thing. Yesterday, I watched this interesting programme, the "50th Anniversary of Television". I watched some of those TV shows in those days, in the early '50s. Compared to what we see today they look so archaic and crude.

Q : How would you want the human species to be if you can...

U.G.: I am not chosen as the guardian spirit or...

Q : I know you are not, but if you could have it the way you would like it, would you...?

U.G.: I like it exactly the way it is. You don't have to do a thing about it. I am not in conflict with this, you see. It cannot be any better. Anything you want to do with this is what creates confusion. So there is violence. As long as you use thought to bring about a change within and a change without, there is bound to be violence. It is bound to be so. Your attempt to create a peaceful state is creating war there.

Q : I forgot...[*Laughs*]

U.G.: Who has given anyone the mandate to change the world?

Q : So you say we are as a species headed towards destruction. Is there a possibility of emerging out of this...?

U.G.: I am not a prophet. But the future is already here.

Q : In what way?

U.G.: In the present. How can it by any different? As I said, through war you cannot create peace in this world.

Q : I wouldn't think so.

U.G.: So, probably we will come to a point where we will be forced by circumstances to live with our adversaries. The way the living organism is functioning – the survival of every cell depends upon the survival of the cell next to it. There is the terror that if I try to destroy something, than I will also go with it. I mean that physically you are going to be destroyed. It will affect you. This terror that if you try to destroy people around you, you are also going to be destroyed with them, may keep us together for a little while now. Certainly it is not love, bliss, worship, or religious thinking. But tell me, why should we be permanent? Why, what for?

Q : Well, that is the question. I don't know.

U.G.: Why? Why are we asking this question?

Q : This probably won't be permanent.

U.G.: We are not concerned. We are not doing anything to keep it permanent. Are we? We are destroying everything there in nature ecologically. Ecological problems have been aggravated by us. How do you think what we are doing will help? Anybody who says anything against exhaust fumes and who is himself driving a car should be shot at sight and on sight. He is also contributing. Don't believe that fellow! All the ecologists, don't believe them.

Q : Because they are not interested?

U.G.: They are not interested in it at all.

Q : Is anyone interested in conserving it?

U.G.: Nobody is interested in it.

Q : Not even you?

U.G.: I am the last person to be interested, because I don't want this to be any different.

Q : It is all very bleak, Sir!

U.G.: It is not bleak. How can you say it is bleak? That is the only thing. So real it is. Not at all bleak. You would like to use that word, fancy phrase, and say it is bleak. Look at that this moment. It's wonderful! [*Both look at the ocean*]. I don't write poetry. The next moment I am looking at you, you are as beautiful as the ocean there. Probably more beautiful. You see, if I am freed from all the ideas that I have of beauty, there is something that is extraordinary there. Nothing needs to be done to change anything. Things are changing in their own ways. Nature is changing – some volcanic eruptions somewhere and some earthquakes somewhere. Why these things occur we don't know. You know, the seismologists can predict with exact precision that we are going to have an earthquake in a particular place at a particular time.

Q : When an asteroid is going to hit us...

U.G.: Why are we all concerned about all these things? – "Who created this world?" "Why de we live?" We leave all these things to the metaphysicians and scientists.

Q : Probably we are afraid of death?

U.G.: We are afraid of coming to an end.

Q : Yes, I don't want to come to an end. Are you afraid of coming to an end?

U.G.: There is nothing 'here' to come to an end.

Q : So that is how we may be different ... I am so concerned about it.

U.G.: Don't say, "Different". Nothing will come to an end except the one that does not want to come to an end. It is interested in preserving itself somehow, in some way, even beyond death. You see, it is not going to succeed. It is not amusing; it is a fact.

Q : Yes, I understand.

TITLES BASED ON THE CONVERSATIONS WITH U.G. KRISHNAMURTI by SMRITI BOOKS

THE COURAGE TO STAND ALONE
Foreword by Mahesh Bhatt

126 pages 140 x 215 mm
ISBN: 81-87967-06-4

There is some compelling purity about him, some way in which he captures a kind of longing that we all seem to have for a genuinely wise human being.

No one in the history of the world has had the courage to blast authority the way he has and yet no one has stared at one's own insignificance as boldly in the eye.

THOUGHT IS YOUR ENEMY
Foreword by Mahesh Bhatt
148 pages 140 x 215 mm
ISBN : 81-87967-11-0

This book is a compilation of discussions between U. G. Krishnamurti and various questioners in India, Switzerland, Australia, Netherlands and U.K. According to U.G., "The religious states of bliss and ecstasy can never be experienced, can never be grasped, contained, much less given expression to, by any man. That beaten track will lead you nowhere. There is no oasis situated yonder; you are stuck with a mirage."

NO WAY OUT
Foreword by Mahesh Bhatt

140 x 215 mm
ISBN : 81-87967-08-0

"Political institutions and ideologies are the warty outgrowth of the religious thinking of the man; in a way responsible for the tragedy of mankind. We are slaves to our ideas and beliefs and torture ourselves in the hope of achieving something. All our experience, spiritual or otherwise is the basic cause of our suffering...the body is not interested in anything 'you' are interested in; that is the battle that is going on all the time. There seems to be no way out!"

THE MYSTIQUE OF ENLIGHTENMENT

Foreword by Mahesh Bhatt

140 x 215 mm
ISBN : 81-87967-09-9

A no- nonsense book about that truth which many spiritual seekers are seeking –what most gurus call 'enlightenment', and what U.G. Krishnamurti calls the 'natural state'. U.G. maintains, in this selection from his conversations, that the so-called enlightenment is a purely biological phenomenon; that only when we are completely free of culture conditioning, religious thinking and intellect, can our body, with its own extraordinary intelligence, get free to be in the 'natural' state. The book is an invaluable roadside companion for all those on the 'path' or thinking of setting out on it. It tells the inside story of a man who knows the 'holy business' from the ground up, and who reveals in a frank and direct manner how he became 'free' not because of, but despite of a lifetime of spiritual practice.

MIND IS A MYTH

Foreword by Mahesh Bhatt

140 x 215 mm
ISBN : 81-87967-10-2

This is the story of a man who had it all—looks, wealth, culture, fame, travel, career—and gave it all up to find for himself the answer to his burning question, "Is there actually anything like freedom, enlightenment or liberation behind all the abstractions the religions have thrown at us?" He never got an answer. The book introduces you to the unknown truth of life.